Killer Business Plan
Why You Need It, How To Write It

Peter and Lydia Mehit

Praise for Killer Business Plan

"A must read for both seasoned entrepreneurs and those brand new to starting a business! By using direct language and clear illustrations, Peter and Lydia Mehit pinpoint what needs to be inside an entrepreneur's head to start and sustain a thriving business each step of the way; beginning with choosing a business, through visualizing its sounds, sights, and smells, to detailing the financial and operational aspects of any given business venture—*Killer Business Plan* gives entrepreneurs worldwide a rock-solid, powerful platform from which to launch their enterprise."

> - *Ivan Misner, Ph.D.,*
> *NY Times Bestselling Author and Founder of BNI®*

"*Killer Business Plan* is more than a practical approach to writing a comprehensive business plan; it is a tool involving worksheets and videos that imbue the reader with practical knowledge to lay the foundation for their business. Peter and Lydia convey in plain (and even at times humorous) English why a business without a strong foundation is guaranteed to work harder than its peers and likely – fail. I highly recommend that entrepreneurs of all experience levels learn that there is a difference between; having no plan, thinking you have a plan, and having a *Killer Business Plan.*"

> - *Virginia Lorimor*
> *Founder of the WIN Companies*

"In *Killer Business Plan*, Peter Mehit has written a very comprehensive book that encompasses much more that just the writing of a business plan. He starts with the basics by asking the reader what business they want to choose and why. From there he talks about visualizing the customer, feasibility models, funding sources, and then he gets to the building of the actual business plan. In other words, his book is a very good example by being a great business plan for a book. I highly recommend this step-by-step manual to launching a successful business."

> – *Boaz Rauchwerger*
> *Author, Speaker and Contributor to Lifetime Network's*
> *'The Balancing Act'*

"The Mehits have crafted a comprehensive, readable treasure chest in their book on writing a killer business plan. There is so much more to this book than mere instruction on the writing of a business plan – they wisely lead the would-be entrepreneur through a sometimes gut wrenching analysis of figuring out what they 'really want' and how to get there. No skirting around the real issues is allowed as you follow the Mehits easy to digest yet immensely challenging program for getting ready to develop, start and run the business of your dreams. I have no doubt that this book can be the decisive element between immense success and abject failure for the budding or seasoned entrepreneur."

> - *Kristin Tillquist,*
> *Author, 'Capitalizing on Kindness: Why 21st Century*
> *Professionals Need to be Nice'.*

"Killer Business Plan is a **"must have"** for everyone starting a business. *Killer Business Plan* is part workbook, part guide, and part advisor – it is like having your own start-up coach walking you through step-by-step. If you want to achieve success consider this book filled with practical, immediately applicable advice your business start-up tour guide."

-   *Michelle Skiljan, Executive Director*
    Inland Empire Women's Business Center

© 2012 Peter and Lydia Mehit
P.O. Box 16115
Irvine, CA 92623-6115

ISBN: 978-1-105-38031-0

First Trade Paperback Edition 2012

Killer Business Plan
Why You Need It, How To Write It

For my uncle, Nicholas Graur, a lifetime entrepreneur. Our times together were brief, but you made an impact that has lasted a lifetime.

- Peter Mehit

To Edith Tibbs, my mother, who gave me everything I need to make it in life, especially love.

- Lydia Mehit

Table of Contents

Acknowledgements

We want to thank a few people whose assistance made this book possible:

Lilia Garcia worked tirelessly on research, drafting and formatting of both the narrative and online segments of this work while bringing joy and humor to our office. Her love and support saw us through this adventure.

Dwayne Miller assisted us in the creation of the online products used in this work along with substantial assistance in a companion product, *'Employee to Entrepreneur'* (www.e2enow.com). His tenacious spirit is in these pages.

Michelle Skiljian and Nicole Kinney of the Inland Empire Woman's Business Center provided countless classroom opportunities for us to present this material and perfect it. They have been an unflagging source of support over the years.

And finally, we thank our clients who taught us everything we know. The insights in this book came from our work with them. We are stronger from participating in their struggles and encouraged by their successes. We have been forever changed by, and are grateful for, the relationships we have made with them.

Introduction

When people consider starting a business, writing a business plan is usually the last thing they think of. It's exciting to dive into details, start choosing paint colors, pricing equipment. Yet starting a business without a plan is like taking a trip to a new locale without a map or building a house without blueprints. You may finish the project, you even get a good result, but the odds are it will take you more time and cost you more money without them.

Your business plan will be written, whether you put fingers to a keyboard or ink to paper. It will be written by the circumstances you experience, the people you listen to, the decisions you make. Your plan can be written by fate with every decision made in real time, where the odds of making the right one approach the probability of a coin toss. Or your business plan can be the product of deliberate choices made after discovery, research and contemplation. But it will be written nonetheless and the choice is up to you.

It makes sense, therefore, to make your plan in advance where you have a chance to consider your path forward, to ponder what can go right and wrong. Having a detailed plan gives you structure, makes you resistant to magical thinking and gives you a perspective where you can understand the consequences of choices made early, where the margin of error is smaller than most realize.

Your plan may have errors, but the rigor of creating it will discipline your mind and expose areas that need reinforcement. You will have a mental picture of your destination and the journey you will take to reach it. This makes trips down dead ends less likely. But most importantly, it keeps you in control instead of being controlled by others that don't share your goals.

There's a school of thought about entrepreneurship that says you need to just get going. If you focus on the product or the customer and make it great, everything else will simply unfold. For most businesses, this is not true. Every product or service you buy has a machine attached to it, *a business*. Not planning that business, its operations, cash flow requirements, how it reaches its customers is akin to relying on miracles.

Imagine if the iPad took twelve weeks to get online instead of an instant purchase in a beautiful store. What if service required repeated UPS trips to a factory? What if the Apple Store Genius Bar was replaced by a group of untrained support slugs in an online forum? How many iPads would be sitting in a warehouse gathering dust?

The success of the iPad is the result of rigorous, detailed planning. Not just the product, but the marketing, the customer experience, service, warranties all the way down to what the employees say to you when you enter the store. Nothing is left to chance. Everything is planned so that what works can be repeated and what doesn't can be corrected. Without a plan, you will only be able to guess why you are succeeding or failing.

Your business plan, then, is the design of the machine that will support your product or service. It is your opportunity to make sure you create the best possible environment for success. It is your chance to make sure the chassis is strong enough, that the engine has enough power to carry your business to your goals.

We have written over five hundred business plans across multiple industries for bank, angel investor and venture funding. Our firm, Custom Business Planning and Solutions, has raised over $75MM in funding for our clients using these plans. We know what a killer business plan can do.

We wrote this book for entrepreneurs who want to truly understand what they are getting into. Starting a business can be the most rewarding thing you can do in your professional life. It can also be the biggest nightmare you've ever lived through. Again, the choice is yours. Plan to succeed.

Peter and Lydia Mehit
Chino Hills, CA

How To Use This Book

Killer Business Plan is presented in three parts:

> *Part 1 – What Business Should I Choose?* is a primer regarding the basic ways you can get into business for yourself. It also discusses the traits common to successful business owners in detail. If you are not sure what business you should get into, or have a limited business background, you would start here.

> *Part 2 – How Much Will My Business Make?* The most important part this section are the feasibility models that are provided for you at the website. Use these models to determine if your business is going to provide the income you desire. If the business isn't likely to produce the cash flow you need, you will know before you've gone through the rigor of producing a full business plan.

> Part 2 also discusses the various corporate structures you can use to operate your business as well as running down the most common funding sources you will use to get started. There is also a discussion regarding non-profits and grants, who uses them and how they work.

> *Part 3 – Create My Business Plan* takes you section by section through creating a killer business plan. The sections are presented in the order we believe will work best for you and will allow you to stop at the earliest point possible if it appears your business idea will not work.

> Numerous examples, videos and templates are provided at *www.killerbusinessplan.com* and they are referenced in the text so you know when to use them. To access them, click on

'Electronic Materials' on the menu bar and enter the password zzx112. Feel free to download and save the tools for your personal use only. We claim them as exempt from the 'Fair Use' doctrine. Contact us if you would like to distribute the materials or use them in a classroom setting at 800-741-8444 or *pmehit@custombps.com.*

Part 1 – What Business Should I Choose?

Overview

"The road to contentment," my uncle Nick said to me when I was young, *"is in knowing what you want."* It sounds simple, but most people have never taken the time to really figure this out. We get so busy doing what we've done before, finding jobs, meeting expectations, keeping other people happy. *What about what we want?*

The funny thing about that question, the less you ask it, the more you don't have an answer. I got my first job so I could buy a car to haul my drums around. It's been several decades since that goal was met and forgotten. I have moved on to other goals, but along the way I've learned to always ask how the step I'm about to take is going to get me where I ultimately want to go.

Since you're reading this, it's safe to assume that you want to change your life by starting a business. You may, or may not, know what that business is and that's no problem. It's more important to figure out what you truly want. Killer Business Plan is designed to do just that.

First things first; If you want to start a business to make money, great. If everything goes perfectly, this may be enough motivation. In our experience, the people who thrive, the ones that make it through tough times, are the ones that have a passion for their work and their customers.

The quickest way to earn money in business, when you don't care about what you do, is a job.

Money is not enough to get you through the challenges you will face.

Part 1 has nine chapters. While you can work the chapters in any order, it is recommended that you complete them in order

Part 1 Consists Of:

Chapter 1: A discussion of the common traits found in entrepreneurs and business owners.

Chapter 2: A discussion of the pros and cons of purchasing a franchise.

Chapter 3: Focuses on what it takes to start a business from scratch.

Chapter 4: An overview of what's involved when purchasing a business, including the different methods of valuation.

Chapter 5: A Decision Document to formalize what you have learned and the decisions you have made.

Chapter 6: Visualizing a 'day in the life' of your business and strategies for collecting ideas and information to realize that vision.

Chapter 7: Identifying the perfect customer(s).

Chapter 8: Part 1 summary.

Chapter 9: A Final Decision Document to formalize what you have learned and the decisions you have made in the part.

Chapter 1 – Know Yourself

The Goal of This Chapter

Discuss the qualities possessed by business owners/entrepreneurs.

What You Will Do in This Chapter

Learn about the importance of understanding your appetite for risk, your willingness to sell and the commitment required to create a successful business.

Create a preliminary list of businesses you are interested in starting.

What You Will Have When You're Done

A good understanding of how you match up against the challenges before you as an entrepreneur.

Background

We've worked with hundreds of clients one on one, and have seen some strange behavior. For example, we had a client who worked in retail but that didn't want to sell to men or work weekends. We've had clients with thousands of customers but couldn't keep their shops full because they wouldn't market to them. We've had business owners who really don't like people go into service businesses and we've seen genuine 'people' people slave away in back offices.

When you think that all these people chose their businesses, it makes you scratch your head and say, "How could you not see yourself?" But it's so common that we created this chapter to discuss it.

It's best expressed this way. The fact that you can perform accounting doesn't mean you're an accountant. You may have had a long series of jobs, or a career in accounting, but that doesn't mean that your heart or head is in it. Choosing a business that plays to what you've always done is smart, but it can't be done to the exclusion of who you are or what you *really* want.

Starting a business is the most difficult and rewarding thing you can do in your work life. It draws on almost every talent you have and requires that you understand yourself in ways that jobs never require. The approaches you used as an employee can sink you as an owner. You will need to be committed like you've never been before. That is why you have to love, *passionately*, the business you are starting. No one will ever work as hard, or care as much, about your enterprise as you.

Most people have never been asked, or even asked themselves what they want. That question can be like the proverbial blank sheet of paper to a person with writer's block. You know the subject, but the words aren't there. The best way to tackle this is to get information, starting with you.

What We Believe

There are only three things an entrepreneur/business owner actually does:

- Predict
- Decide
- Execute

Below are traits we believe are common to successful business people. It's important to remember that while these are traits common to successful people, you don't have to have a specific personality to succeed. Your success will be as individual as you are.

IMPORTANT: The profiles we discuss below are *very generalized guidelines* and are not exhaustive. Further, there is nothing to say you can't change any beliefs you don't like. It's also possible that we are making statements in a way that doesn't work for you. Don't get hung up. Take these profiles as a *starting point.*

Risk Profile

The number one thing that stops most people from going into business for themselves is risk tolerance. The spectrum of risk runs from the daredevil who laughs at any consequence to the phobic who won't leave the house. Between these two points are an infinite number of positions that collect, in bell curve like fashion, around a center point of indecision.

What does indecision have to do with risk tolerance? Most people have a very difficult time making decisions. Most don't and let the situation dictate the outcome. Others collect endless information with the hope that the sheer volume of information will make a decision easier and sometimes, it does. Often, it just creates more confusion. There are a thousand ways to avoid making a decision: It's too early, it's too late, we don't have the time, or the money, or…. You get it.

Indecision kills. A key skill for growth is the ability to make timely decisions. That ability is tied into our beliefs about risk. If you are risk averse, you will lean toward indecisiveness, and that is not good for a business owner.

Commitment Profile

The second major factor that can derail business success is commitment. Commitment is a measure of how much time and effort you're willing to put into your business. Unlike a movie, where all the hard work passes by in a montage set to driving rock music, your passage to success will be marked with storms, ambivalent successes, spectacular failures and tedium. It's exactly like life but instead you're calling the shots. We have found that people who are unable or unwilling to put in the effort will fail.

Does being committed mean you will succeed? It's hard to fail when you refuse to give up. So, while it isn't a guarantee for success, lack of commitment is a sure precursor to failure.

Resource Profile

When we speak of resources in the context of this chapter, we mean everything external to you, although, from reading what we just covered, you can see that what's in your head is a resource too. Resources, for the purposes of this program are:

- People who will be your customers or can bring customers to you
- An understanding of your competition and how to beat them
- Reasonable credit, assets and/or access to capital
- Relationships with people who can and will help you advance your business
- Willingness to explore assumptions and accept criticism
- Ability to partner with others

Are these all the resources you need? Of course not, but it's our best effort to get at whether you have enough to justify the time and energy required to pursue your business idea.

Selling Profile

No one will ever be as passionate or a better salesman for your company than you. It is nice to think that you can hire talent to make the sale, but the truth is you will have to sell your company to the salesman first. Great sales people can only sell what they believe in. That means they have to believe in you and your ideas in order to succeed.

If you've had a job, a spouse or gotten your kids to clean up their rooms, you know how to sell. As an owner you just do it on purpose.

In the beginning of almost any enterprise, you will be doing a lot of selling. You'll be selling to investors, banks or friends and family to get money, selling to suppliers to get good terms or delivery slots, to commercial real estate brokers for retail space and finally, after all that selling, you'll get to sell to your customers.

In fact, if you aren't selling, you're not in business. Selling is the most important thing you do; what you sell is irrelevant if you can't find customers and close the deal.

Let that sink in for a minute. If you think you're going to be able to launch a business, make fabulous sums of money and not sell people on your ideas and products, then it is my task to introduce you to the world of the real. Selling is not the domain of the car salesman or telemarketer striving to push things onto people they don't want or need. Selling, in the context of this program, is a method of communicating value to a prospective customer so they can make their own buying decision.

People Profile

You're a people person or you're not. Luckily, you don't have to be a people person to succeed at business, but it does have some bearing on what kind of business you get into. If you don't like dealing with people, opening a bed and breakfast would probably be a bad idea. If you like working with people or find strangers fascinating, then being a computer systems designer could make you nuts. It's important that you understand your temperament in this area because it will affect your success.

Creating a Preliminary List of Businesses

The roadblock for most people is not deciding to start their own business, (that decision is easy) but deciding which business to start (hmmm, maybe not so easy). Should you start a business like the one you're currently working in as an employee? Should you start a service business? Should you start a retail business? Should you take Grandma's recipe that everyone loves and create an internet business?

Here is a technique to use that can help:

Find a quiet spot, get a notepad and ask yourself some simple questions. There is no rush, take your time and really think about the answers, and answer as honestly as you can.

1. Imagine all businesses were created equal. They all pay one dollar a day. What can you see your self doing? In other words, if money didn't matter, what kind of life do you see yourself leading?

2. What do you do that people compliment you on?

3. What awards or achievements have you received in your life that gave you special pleasure? What did you do that brought you that recognition?

4. Recall several of your most recent pleasurable experiences. What things were common across them?

Write down your answers and all of the ideas you are considering on paper. You think you'll remember but it's easy to forget and writing things down frequently helps clarify your thoughts.

Now you have a preliminary list of businesses you would be interested in starting. Put the list aside for a moment. We'll get back to it in Chapter 5.

Chapter 2 - Franchises

The Goal of This Chapter

Learn some of the benefits of owning a franchise.
Learn the steps to researching a franchise.
Learn the questions to ask before buying.

What You Will Do in This Chapter

You will read the information on franchises to see if this type of business is right for you.

What You Will Have When Completed

You will have a basic understanding of how franchises work.
You will have enough knowledge to begin researching a franchise.

To Franchise or Not to Franchise

There are two ways to buy a franchise. You can purchase a new franchise from the franchisor, or you can purchase one from an existing franchisee, which will require the approval of the franchisor. It doesn't matter which method you choose, the benefits of ownership are nearly the same. The principles discussed in Chapter 4, "Buying a Business" should be reviewed if you are purchasing an existing business.

Benefits of a Franchise:

1. Proven business model (if it is a well established franchise)

2. Pre defined target market

3. Proven track record of successful stores (if not, move on)

4. Known product or service (brand recognition)

5. Access to proprietary business methods and systems

6. Management training provided

7. Faster startup, shorter learning curve (everything is laid out for you, fewer decisions to make)

8. On the job training is provided for your staff, your manager and you

9. Operations manual that details all of the job descriptions, processes, procedures, rules and requirements for operating the business is provided

10. Store layout design help

11. Assistance selecting a suitable location and negotiating the lease

12. Equipment lists and purchase sources identified and prices negotiated

13. Vendors identified (the collective buying power of the franchisor can allow for bulk buys with savings passed to franchisees)

14. Assistance negotiating leases for equipment

15. Marketing plan already developed, help with advertising materials or advertising provided by the franchise

16. SBA lenders favor franchises (*if* they are on the SBA approved list)

NOTE: Not all franchises offer all of the above benefits. Your research will reveal what is available for a particular franchise.

Disadvantages of Buying a Franchise:

1. Strict operational requirements- Most franchisors require you run your business in specific ways, even down to the details of how the fixtures are placed and the product displayed.

2. The initial franchisee fee - for a nationally known franchise the fee can range from $35K to $1MM. You still have to lease or purchase a building, renovate it, furnish it, and if you are opening a retail business, purchase inventory. The additional cost of the franchise fee could make the startup capital requirements difficult to finance.

3. Royalties-Besides the initial franchise fee, you will be paying a percentage of your business revenue (royalties) to the franchisor every month. This amount ranges from 3-10%. This amount is usually taken from gross revenue, which means that the franchise takes its cut *before* you cover your expenses.

4. Advertising royalties-You may be required to pay an additional 2-5% of your gross sales to the franchise for use in national or regional advertising.

5. Territories-You will have geographic boundaries to your business. You may only be able to market and advertise within your assigned territory. This territory designation could be a city or a neighborhood. Be sure you understand how the franchisor develops territory boundaries. Make sure they are drawn in a consistent manner.

6. You will be restricted to buying your product, supplies and equipment from designated vendors, and sometimes from the franchisor. You will not be able to gain economies and lower overhead by shopping around.

7. You will only be able, in most cases, to sell items specified by the franchisor.

8. Limited geographical area-Not all franchises will have territories available convenient to you. You may have to locate your business in the next city or county to get the franchise you want.

9. The separation agreement- may contain punitive clauses. You may be barred from working in the same or similar business for a specified period of time after your contract expires. So, if you owned a sandwich shop franchise, and you thought you could do it better and cheaper outside of the franchise, you would be unable to open a sandwich shop after your contract expired for two or more years.

10. Term-most agreements are for 10 years. That is a long time if the franchise turns out not to be what you thought. Choose carefully!

11. The franchisor's problems are also your problems. Carefully check their financial stability and reputation.

12. Loss of control-most franchisors impose price, appearance and design requirements. You will have limited to no ability to innovate.

13. One may not be enough-you may only be able to make a profit comparable to the annual salary of a good job, $50 - 75K. If your financial goals are larger, you may have to purchase additional locations or territories to reach them.

Franchise Brokers

A franchise broker can help you select a franchise based on your skills, interests and available cash to invest. They may also make referrals to lenders, and help you fill out the franchise applications and accompanying paperwork.

Things to Consider

1. Many franchise brokers work for the franchise and only get paid if a sale is completed.

2. Some brokers' compensation is a percentage of the cost of the franchise, so be sure they are not steering you to a higher priced franchise.

3. Some brokers may have a limited pool of franchises they promote and as such you will not be presented with a large variety of choices to review.

4. Sadly, compensation drives behavior. It's important, before you begin, to know how the broker is paid, and to pay attention to the choices presented to you.

Evaluating a Franchise

Remember to look at all opportunities in light of your goals and personal preferences. A franchise is not the right choice for everyone, which is why a large percentage of franchisees sell their franchise before the end of the agreement.

This is a long term relationship. You must take great care when selecting a franchise.

If you think a franchise may be for you and plan to investigate further, here are some things you might want to consider.

1. If the franchise is a family-owned or closely held business and the franchisor has placed relatives in key roles, be sure they are qualified for their positions and have the experience to keep the franchise successful.

2. You will likely have a designated territory, but only in regards to other franchisees. This means the franchisor can open a company store in your territory whenever they choose. Try to get this clause removed from the agreement. Make sure you understand the rules regarding this.

3. If you are required to purchase supplies from the franchisor or from a preselected vendor, be sure their rates are competitive. Paying above market prices for your supplies or product erodes your profit margin.

4. Beware of making an emotional purchase based on your personal preferences for a product or service. Do your research to be sure it is a good business opportunity and that it suits your skills.

5. If it is a fairly new franchise, ask why they decided to franchise as opposed to expanding their business by opening additional locations or licensing. Find out how many locations they had before they decided to franchise their business model.

6. If it is a small franchise, talk to every franchisee you can before purchasing. A small franchise is like becoming part of a family, so you want to know everything about them.

7. If a franchisor is overly enthusiastic about signing you up without in depth knowledge of your skills, qualifications and financial backing, be cautious. Most franchisors are very selective, and look for the best qualified candidates who possess both the skills and capital needed to succeed.

A resource for you is the Federal Trade Commission (FTC) web site. They have a publication written for consumers purchasing a franchise. Go to *www.ftc.gov* and put the word franchise in the search box. "Buying a Franchise: A Consumer Guide" should display on the first page of the search results.

Making a Short List

You've found two or three franchises that may fit the bill. They match your interests, your life style and your skills. They are within your budget and you can see yourself successfully operating any one of them. You've navigated all the issues above and are comfortable with the information you've received.

Excellent, you've made a good start. Now you need to take an in-depth look at your finalists.

1. Do your research.

2. READ the Franchise Disclosure Document (FDD). Reading an FDD can be like chewing a tar sandwich, but you're getting married for 10 years or more. You need to know what you're getting. So let me say it again. Read the Franchise Disclosure Document. Repeat until you're sure your understand it.

3. Interview franchisees, past and present. By law the FDD should include contact information for franchisees that have left the system.

4. Find out how the franchise is perceived by others in the same industry.

5. Is the franchise well respected, or are people surprised they're still in business?

Below you will find a few key points you should be sure to cover during your in-depth look at a franchise you are considering purchasing.

1. Assess your risk and the financial return prior to signing. Understand how much money you will make and the effort, in time and money, you will have to invest. *Beware: franchise pro-forma financial statements are normalized and may not reflect your local experience. It would be prudent to do your own pro-forma projections using information specific to your part of the country and potential customer pool.*

2. Compare the franchise you are investigating to others in the same market segment. Do they look better, the same or worse than their competition?

3. Pay special note to the clauses in the contract that may restrict your ability to sell your business. Most contracts are for an initial term of 10 years and *most franchisees will leave the business before the term is completed.* Plan for the best, prepare for the worst.

4. As with all important documents in your business life, have an attorney look over the agreement before you sign. A good attorney, even at $300 per hour is inexpensive insurance.

5. If the franchise requires you to pay a marketing royalty for national advertising, be sure the franchise advertises regularly in your region of the country. If they don't advertise in your locale try to negotiate the fees out of your agreement.

6. Although some franchisors will tell you the FTC doesn't allow them to speak about the financial performance of their franchises, *there is no such restriction.* They cannot guarantee that you will make the same revenues as the other franchisees, but they can tell you what the other stores are grossing in general terms. Push them to reveal hard numbers. If they won't talk numbers, they should tell you about trends their franchisees are experiencing. Ask, "Are same store sales trending up, flat or down from last year to this year?"

7. How do current franchisees feel about the franchisor; are they enthusiastic and feel well treated, or do they have open issues that need to be resolved?

8. Listen carefully as you interview franchisees. Is there open communication with the franchisor? Will you be able to talk to managers or get help over the phone from the corporate office? Do franchisees feel informed? *It's a very positive sign when the franchisor encourages you to visit franchisees unaccompanied.*

9. Talk to franchisees to find out how long it will take to be profitable.

10. Try to spend a full day (better yet, several days) with a franchisee to find out what they are doing to be successful and how they spend their time. This will also give you a good idea of what your life will be like once you start your business. Make sure you can visualize yourself doing this every day.

Chapter 3 - Start Ups

The Goal of This Chapter

Help you decide if you want to build a business from the ground up.

What You Will Do in This Chapter

Complete homework assignments to help you decide if you want to build your business from scratch.

What You Will Have When You're Done

You will understand the benefits and the drawbacks of building your business from the ground up.

Starting a Business from Scratch

What does this mean exactly? It means, you select your own location, you decide if you will lease or purchase the building, you lay out the design of the space yourself, you select your inventory and choose your own suppliers, you design your business model, you decide how many employees you need and their positions, you write the job descriptions. In other words, you figure it all out.

Many people think, "Build it and they will come." **NOT TRUE!!!** If you believe this, you are dreaming. They will only come if:

1. They know you are there
2. Understand what you are offering
3. Have a need for your product or service
4. Are willing to pay the price you're charging.

Many people start their business from scratch because they believe they have the latest and greatest idea anyone has ever seen and is sure everyone wants it. Others think, "How hard can it be? I know this product or service inside and out, surely I can make a success of a business".

Regardless of your thought process, while your business is still an idea in your mind, you should identify your target customer and start asking if they need or want your product or service. Even if it is obvious that there is a pressing need, you still want to find out how your potential customers want it packaged, priced and delivered.

Don't start your business in the blind. Find out what your potential customers will buy and how they want to buy it before you start.

How will you do this? There are many ways to discover this information including surveys and communications with family, friends and your target customer. Reading news and reports on your subject from trade magazines, newspapers and internet sources will also be valuable. Introduce your subject at social events and listen to the comments. Don't argue or defend your idea, just find out what people think of it.

At minimum, you should do the following informal research:

1. Talk with your family and friends about your idea. Try not to be defensive if they question you, and listen closely to what they have to say.
2. Identify the most likely consumer for your product or service.
3. Talk to several potential consumers to find out if they would buy
4. Ask if they would prefer to purchase over the internet, in-person or from a sales person
5. Ask how would they buy; in bulk, one at a time, in packages of two, etc.
6. Ask how much they would be willing to pay
7. Find out how and where they would expect it see it advertised

Once you think you have a saleable product or service, set your goals and put them in writing. Once you know where you want to go, you can make a plan to get there.

Write a business plan. **If you fail to plan, you are planning to fail**. The business plan will help you uncover areas you may not have considered previously. It will clarify your thinking and allow you to respond quickly when making business decisions. It will organize your thinking, reveal priorities and set you on the road to success.

Your business plan will benefit you as you build and grow your business, but it will also benefit you before you open the business. As you talk to others about your business including bankers, investors, potential partners, potential employees and landlords, your business plan, or parts of it, can be used to illustrate points and to clarify your intentions.

- Detail your product or service and how you will operate your business.
- Pin point your target customers, find out where they live and how you will reach them. Figure out how many sales you need to get the income you desire.

  o Is it a reasonable number?
  o Can you reach the number by your 2nd or 3rd year in business or more importantly before you run out of working capital?
  ▪ Research your business idea.
  o You will find out if there is a large enough market for your product or service.
  o You will familiarize yourself with the competition and the current price point.
  o You will expand your knowledge on who will buy and why.

Now that you know there is a need for your product or service, you know who will purchase it, and you know how much they are willing to pay for it. There are still a few things you want to consider before you create your business.

Before you start: Make sure you have your finances in order. A major failing of start up businesses is lack of sufficient capital. Don't be a statistic.

- Pay off or reduce as much debt as possible before you start

- Review your credit record to see if you can improve your credit score
- Have money in the bank for living expenses until your business makes money
- Keep your start-up capital separate from the money for your living expenses

Plan your transition from employee to entrepreneur by considering your living expenses and having a back up plan for them, including child care and health insurance.

Get professional advice as needed from accountants/CPAs, financial planners, business consultants, bankers and lawyers. Don't go it alone, develop a support network of professionals, mentors, friends and colleagues to take advantage of their wisdom, guidance and connections. They can help you navigate the rough spots you will encounter.

Talk to your family to find out how they feel about you starting a business. Support from your family and significant other is crucial to your success. *If your loved ones feel abandoned, no success will be enough.*

Start part-time, if possible, while at your current job. This will allow you to cover your expenses while you gain experience.

Benefits of a Start-up

- There are no predetermined rules or formulas to follow; it's all up to you.
- Personal growth/enhanced skills including public speaking and decision making
- Tax advantages – items that are purchased for business purposes are tax deductible (keep your receipts).
- The owner is in control of all aspects of the business including the location and what the operation will look like
- The entrepreneur may draw from previous job experience, skills and passion in establishing the business.
- Many businesses may be started in your spare time; you can either moonlight while at your current job, so you can test your idea while you still have income, or you can

consider cutting your full time job to part time and dedicate the additional time to your new business. You would not be able to start small like this if you purchase a franchise or an existing business.

Disadvantages of a Start-up

- Capital needs are more difficult to predict and capital may be more difficult to obtain because your business doesn't have a track record
- You will have to do everything yourself from marketing and sales to cleaning the shop and collecting accounts
- You have to learn everything very quickly or have enough money to hire people to support you in the various areas
- You have to become an expert at prioritizing your actions and pacing your work load as you learn your new business
- There are no predetermined rules or formulas to follow; it's all up to you.

Chapter 4 - Buying a Business

The Goal of This Chapter

Give you information to help you decide if you wish to purchase a business.

What You Will Do in This Chapter

Complete research to help you decide if you want to purchase an existing business or franchise.

What You Will Have When You're Done

You will be aware of the main advantages and disadvantages of purchasing an existing business. You will have an idea of how to evaluate if this business is for you and how to estimate for yourself if the asking price is realistic.

Buying a Business

There are many good reasons why buying an existing business could make sense for you. Buying an ongoing business will provide you with benefits not found in a start up or a franchise, like immediate cash flow. Understand that you will need to put time and effort into finding a business that is right for you and it is likely you will have several false starts before finding the right one.

In the following paragraphs we touch on the advantages and disadvantages of purchasing a business and some things to consider once you've selected a business to buy. This is a large purchase and whether you do it alone or use a business broker to support you through the process, you should educate yourself before you begin.

Advantages

- Immediate cash flow from existing customers and receivables
- A market for the product or service has already been established
- Established customer base
- Established reputation in the community
- The financial history, if positive, will help you get funding
- Existing employees will have experience you can draw on.

Disadvantages

- Initial acquisition cost is usually higher than a start up
- The business may have hidden problems such as uncollectable receivables
- You will need to honor or try to renegotiate any contracts the previous owner has in place
- You are subject to the existing perceptions of the business
- Owner may only be available for a limited transition
- Difficult to relocate or rebrand
- Existing systems may not be sufficient to allow growth, if there are even systems in place

While you are searching for a business, keep in the forefront of your mind these questions:

- "Is the business suitable for ME"?
- Whether it is a sole proprietorship or a LLC, or a 'C' corporation, is the legal structure acceptable to you?
- Is there a manager in place, or is this a hands-on business?
- Are you comfortable with the methods and/or hours of operation? (Would you be comfortable if the business opens at 5:00AM, or closes after midnight or is open seven days a week?)
- Analyze your management skills in terms of the number of employees, volume of sales, etc., of the target business.
- Is the purchase price within your means?
- Determine your investment level and an acceptable ROI (return on investment).
- Can you live with what can't be changed about the business?

Now you've selected a business, let the negotiations begin! Right?

Hold on, there's more work ahead. You need to be sure the business is as advertised and that it will provide you with the income you expect. Here are some things to look for before you sign that deal.

Once you select a business:

- Do market research and a competitive analysis to see if it will be a viable choice. Look at where the industry is trending, does the business have the potential to lead or follow the trend, or will it require an additional cash injection if the trend develops as expected.

- Does the business depend on foot traffic to survive? If so, is the location good or is the large anchor tenant of the location pulling out and taking customers with them? If visibility isn't important, consider how close the business is to its customers. Is the target customer within a convenient radius of the business or does it take expensive advertising dollars to capture their attention because they are further away.

- Consider the reasons for sale – talk to people who are familiar with the company and other business owners in the area, don't take the reason the seller gives you at face value.

- Does the business have a good reputation in the community, with its vendors, with the landlord and with their customers? Don't take the current owner's word for it, ask around.

- What is the seller's discretionary cash flow?

    o This number is typically made up of net income, owner's draw, perks, depreciation, interest and non recurring expenses. Typically, these are called 'add backs' because they are added back to a company's earnings to give a buyer a true picture of what they can expect.

    o Confirm the make up of the seller's discretionary cash flow number

- Find out what is included in the asking price. Do not assume you know. Get a detailed list from the owner of equipment, furniture, vehicles, inventory, supplies, office equipment, etc., that is included when you purchase the business. This will keep surprises to a minimum when you take possession of the business.

- Review all liabilities and assets that may be included to determine their exact value.

- Are the assets free of debt? If not, can you still make a profit if you assume the liabilities?

- If you are borrowing money to purchase the business, can you still make a profit after debt service?

- Review the income statements over the past three years with your CPA or other financial professional. Ask the seller to explain declines in profitability or inconsistent items.

- Note the capital requirements of the business. Is it a capital intensive business where equipment requires replacing on a regular basis? Will there be sufficient time before the next round of replacements to acquire the funds from cash flow?

- If there are employees that are crucial to the operations of the business, will they remain after the change in ownership? Are they open to employment contracts?

- How much time will the owner spend with you while the business transitions to you? How much time will the owner give to you after you have taken full possession of the business?

- Evaluate the business to see if you and the owner are close in what you think the business is worth.

Thoroughly investigate all available documentation include accounting records, if possible, before making an offer, and be sure the offer is contingent on a successful due diligence.

Valuing a Business

Understand that valuing a business is not a science but an art and remember that **the asking price is not the purchase price.** Knowing how to value a business is a necessary skill to have when you're shopping for a business to purchase. You must have a method for deciding what the business is worth so when you enter negotiations, you have a firm foundation to support your offer price. There are multiple ways to calculate the value of a business; a few of them are discussed below.

You can calculate the value of a business using:

Asset valuations – calculate the value of all the assets of a business, less depreciation, and arrive at a price. If you are purchasing a small business, this method may not work well for you. For example, a business can be asset rich, but doesn't make much money. How valuable is the business under these circumstances? When the value of a business is determined using this method, the resulting purchase is called an asset sale.

Liquidation value – determine the value of the company's assets if it were forced to sell all of them in a short period of time (usually less than 12 months). The seller is not likely to accept the price calculated by this method, as it will generally be the lowest possible price.

Income Capitalization - future income is calculated based upon historical data and a variety of assumptions. Income capitalization is generally applicable to large businesses.

Rule of Thumb – the selling price of other "like or similar" businesses is used as a multiple of cash flow or a percentage of revenue. The Rule of Thumb method may be too general as it could be hard to find any two businesses for sale that are exactly the same but it is a good place to start when you are trying to develop 'ball park' numbers.

Revenue multiple- the gross sales of a company multiplied by .7 to 2 times. This is a fairly common valuation method. Common multiples for various types of businesses are available from many sources. For example, Inc. magazine publishes a list annually.

Income Multiple – the net income (profit after expenses and taxes) of a business times a factor ranging from a one to four times multiple. Income multiple method is a good method for the purchaser of a small business to use. This tells you what you can expect to have available from the business based on what it has generated in the past.

How do you decide the income multiple? If the owner is the business (if this is a operation where the owner is very active in the business and when the owner leaves so do all of his relationships with customers and vendors that have been built up over time) then you would want to use one to one and a half times income as the multiple. This would be for one-man businesses, small consulting businesses and professional practices. If the customers expect the owner to be available to them most of the time, and know him by name, then they frequent the business based on a relationship with the owner. When the owner sells, they may not be as loyal (if at all) to the new owner.

If the business has a strong track record, repeat clients, a historical pattern of growth, more than 3 years in business, possibly has some proprietary item, or has an exclusive territory or if the business is in a growing industry, it will sell for 2 times earnings or more. Others will fall in between.

Due Diligence

A thorough due diligence is usually performed between reaching a tentative agreement and closing the transaction. Once you have arrived at a preliminary price and terms with the seller, you need to begin your due diligence. There are traditionally three types of due diligence you should do and you might want different advisors for each.

Legal due diligence can determine if the owner has the legal right to sell the business, owns all of the assets, has no legal proceedings against the business and has followed all the regulatory requirements. All of the contracts and leases are also reviewed here.

Financial due diligence consists of double checking the numbers to ensure there are no hidden financial issues or areas not addressed by the documentation you have been previously provided.

Commercial due diligence focuses on the business' place in the marketplace. You should check out the competition comparing price points, products and services, and their proximity to the business you're buying. You should also ensure there are no regulatory issues on the horizon that could negatively impact the business after you purchase it.

You must thoroughly investigate the accounting records and all available documentation before making a final decision

Here is a sample of some of the items reviewed during a typical due diligence period:

- You or your attorney will study the contracts, leases and other documents before you confirm or assume them
- Review the lease, the time left and options for renewal, talk to the landlord
- Review the customer data base against the sales to see how many customers are active and how often they purchase
- Identify key suppliers and ask if they will continue doing business with you under the same terms should you buy the business, or will they be open for negotiation
- Review income statements over the past three years and compare these against the tax returns filed
- Make sure inventory is not obsolete or approaching a "sell by" or other affectivity date
- Check if the equipment and systems are in the condition reported and if they were regularly serviced and maintained
- Check for outstanding gift cards and corresponding allowances to cover them
- Make sure you understand the warranties or guarantees for products sold and confirm their corresponding financial allowances to cover them
- If there is a business plan, study it carefully to become familiar with:

    o How are goods/services delivered?
    o How do they obtain customers?
    o What are the future plans for the business?

- Most importantly, has the business been run in accordance with the plan and if not, why did management deviate from the plan?
  - You might ask permission to sit in on the business for a few days. This will give you a good idea of what it would be like to run the operation.

Chapter 5 - Decision Document 1

The Goal of This Chapter

Shorten the list of business ideas
Complete Decision Document 1

What You Will Do in This Chapter

Review your list of businesses in light of the information in chapters 2, 3 and 4.

After reading the instructions that follow, complete Decision Document 1. The intention of this document is to make a record of the decisions you've made about yourself and your business choice.

What You Will Have When You're Done

A reduced list of possible businesses under consideration
A completed Decision Document

Narrowing the List

Remember that list of business ideas we did way back in Chapter 1? Pull it out once again and review it in light of the information you have read about franchises, startups and purchasing an existing business. Does the new information cause you to eliminate some ideas or add additional ones?

If you have a long list of business ideas, an easy way to shorten the list is to take the first two business ideas and compare them. Which one can you clearly see yourself doing and which one not so much? Eliminate the one that lost. Take the next two and do the same thing. Go through the list and compare every two business ideas, eliminating one of them if possible.

The next step is to review each idea on your list and consider who would be the target of your product or service. In other words, who would benefit if you launched this business? Would you serve the elderly, commuters, young mothers, business owners, blue collar workers, female corporate executives, stay-at-home Dads, or newly retired baby boomers? The more specific you can be the better.

Once you've identified your target audience, ask yourself the following three questions:

1. Am I solving a problem or satisfying a pressing need they have?

2. Does this group of people have the **ability** to pay a fair price for my product or service? (They may want your product or service, but if your idea targets young families, their budget may not stretch to cover the extra expense.)

3. Will this group of people be **willing** to spend their hard-earned money on my product or service? (Whether they have limited or excessive discretionary income, would they spend it in this way?)

Your next step is to take your business ideas to an informal focus group of family, friends and colleagues who you trust and feel know you well, to get their opinions. Be sure to ask your focus groups pointed questions about the perceived value of your product or service, and how much they would be willing to pay (if at all) to receive it.

Remember, if you are thinking of a business to consumer model, people purchase a product or service for three main reasons;

*   To satisfy a basic need
*   To solve a problem
*   To make themselves feel better (this is an emotional driver, not a logical one)

If you are considering a business to business model, the main reason businesses buy products or services are to solve problems that allow them to;

- Increase revenue
- Maintain status quo
- Decrease expenses

Once you have the opinions of your focus group, review the list again and begin to make some decisions. Be open to the opinions of your focus group. Some of what they say may surprise you and some of it you may not like hearing, but listen closely and take their opinions under consideration.

Decision Document Instructions

I have decided to explore businesses in the following areas: *- We are hoping that you will look at your passions and desires and begin getting specific. For example, if you think that you could start a business from scratch and you know that you want to start a restaurant, then write, "I want to start a restaurant, serving American food and I want to make $200,000 per year personally doing it." Be as specific as you can be about your vision at this point. We will be spending more time discussing how to vision your business later.*

I have examined my self and found the following areas I need to focus on: *- Hopefully, the readings have raised areas you may want to reinforce. Write down these knowledge gaps, tendencies or behaviors in this space. If you have an idea of what you are going to do to meet these challenges, then indicate that as well. For example, 'I'm afraid to sell because I don't want people to tell me no.' To overcome this and gain confidence, seek sales training.*

I think the next steps I need to take are: *- These are next steps on any front. It's important that you date when the step is due and then make your best efforts to complete the step by its due date.*

Signature: *- You are creating a contract with yourself. When you sign on the line, you are committing to fulfill your obligations under it. It is a sacred trust. Don't take this lightly. You will become who you want to be when you honor the commitments you make to yourself.*

Decision Document 1

I have decided to explore businesses in the following areas:

_____

_____

_____

_____

_____

I have examined my self and found the following areas I need to focus on:

_____

_____

_____

_____

_____

I think the next steps I need to take are:

Item   Date

_____

_____

_____

_____

_____

I affirm by my signature that I will accomplish the steps I have decided I need to take by the due dates specified.

Signature   **Date**

_____

Chapter 6 - Visualizing Your Business

The Goal of This Chapter

Understand that visualizing your business will help you build it.

What You Will Do in This Chapter

Learn how to envision your business.

Understand how your personality factors into your success.

What You Will Need

A notebook to capture your ideas

Glue Stick

Scissors

An alert and open mind

What You Will Have When You're Done

A vision of your business.

A good understanding of the challenges you will face during start up.

Visualization

"Where there is no vision, the people perish" is a well known biblical quote. But like a lot of other wisdom it isn't as appreciated as it might be.

Our minds excel at pattern recognition. We look for how things fit together, how things work. In fact, our entire existence unfolds from the things we know and believe, along with our experiences.

This is why imagination and visualization are important. When we visualize a future outcome or goal, we are in fact loading our blueprint for how we want the future to unfold. When we break down this vision into goals, we give ourselves targets to shoot for. These are milestones on the journey of making our vision a reality.

We cannot get anywhere without a specific goal. Everything we do is goal driven, from getting a sandwich to making a million. We set our course in life using a series of goals whether we are aware of it or not.

Since we are already using goals in a passive, unconscious way, what would happen if we took a more active role in choosing our goals? How far could we get if we set our destination and let that determine all of the smaller goals in between? It seems deceptively simple but that is the process you need to follow to successfully launch or grow your business, or to accomplish anything else, for that matter.

By not starting with a goal it's easy to lose focus. You may be swayed by people or events into a business that you don't have a passion for. Without a clear goal in mind you may make choices that ultimately lead you away from your desired outcome.

When we let it, our mind can accomplish almost anything. Just add a goal plus commitment and GO! Literally, like a guided missile, it will course correct, continuously refining our course until we reach our target.

Buying a Car

Let's say you're going to buy a car. You decide you will trade in your current car, you want the car to be fuel efficient and you don't want your monthly payment to be more than $350 per month. Now you ready to purchase car; but are you really?

If you stop here there are many things left unconsidered. Do want new or used? What make and model? What options do you want the vehicle to have? There are many unanswered questions, yet you are already shopping.

As you drive along you pass car dealer after car dealer and you feel increasingly confused. Which one will you stop at, which one has the car you're looking for? Your criteria are not detailed enough to allow you to identify the best car for your circumstances and you will give the salesman the power to steer your choice? Without a clear picture of the car you want to purchase, you will waste time and energy and either not get a car, or get the wrong car.

The secret in goal setting is imagining, or envisioning, the end state. What will success look like? This is important because if you haven't visualized your destination, you won't know when you've arrived.

Aim High

As you work toward your goal, you will have incidents that take your project off course and slow it down. You may not get all the funding you need, people in the project may leave or experience set backs; any of a host of things can happen that will cause you fall short of your ultimate goal. If your goal was set at the minimum acceptable outcome and if you fall short, you will probably consider that a failure.

Imagine, however, that you set your sights way beyond that minimally acceptable point and your shot, while not reaching that far goal, flies right past the minimum outcome. Wouldn't that landing spot be more acceptable than falling short?

When putting a golf ball, an instructor tells you to hit the ball hard enough to reach the cup. If enough force is not put into the shot, it can be perfectly straight but not accomplish the goal because it will fall short.

Imagining a larger goal gives you a bigger mental target to hit and your thinking will become more expansive to hit it.

Journal

Most good designers journal. They accumulate their ideas and things they see in the environment that influence them. Writers also do likewise. Having a journal can bring to mind things you've seen, questions you've asked, decisions you've made.

Keeping a journal with you allows you to not worry about whether you'll remember how that one store, you thought was cool, was set up. Your journal, in the sense that we mean it, is more of an idea collector than a book of writings.

What should I put in my journal? - Absolutely anything and every thing. Colors, paint chips, sketches, notes: anything that will help you synthesize the vision of your new business. While a book full of notes may be helpful, a journal that has clippings from magazines, pasted in photos of potential locations and catalog cuts of equipment you will need will be much more stimulating when you are thinking about your business and what it should look, smell and feel like.

Clustering, a writing technique that is remarkably adaptable to a number of other endeavors is something you should learn about. You start with a single idea and then link it to related ideas, without requiring that things have structure or make sense right away.

As you can see in the example at right, many related topics to the word 'doll house' are clustered around various main idea words. The idea is to accumulate enough ideas on the page that the ones that move you will become obvious to you. If you do the same 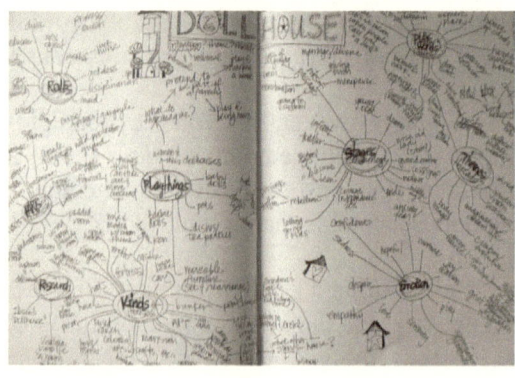 thing with color combinations, shapes, spaces and so on, you give your sub-conscious, creative mind more options to ponder.

It may seem at first that you are giving yourself too much information, but over time (and rather quickly, we might add) patterns in your preferences will emerge, making choices easier. we cannot emphasize this enough. If the first time you are thinking about the color of the walls of your space or whether your equipment should be chrome or matte black is when you are meeting with a salesman to order it, unless you are a very decisive person, you can be thrown into something near a crisis. Not knowing where you're going creates unnecessary stress. It can undermine your confidence, or worse, make you vulnerable to sales people who are motivated by the size of the order, not your best interests.

Keep your journal with you. All the time. Everyday. Inspiration will strike more frequently if you do. You will learn how to make your journal work for you. No two are alike. There is no right or wrong way, just *your* way.

Step 1: Visit the Destination

When you are thinking about your business idea, a helpful thing to do is imagine what a day in the business will be like. This will bring your idea into sharper focus and help you stay motivated as you move towards its realization.

The examples that follow are intended as a guide. Don't be hung up on the order of the examples, jump in where it feels right.

In your notebook, reserve a chapter for your *'Day In The Life'* visioning. You should set aside enough pages so the writing can expand as much as it needs to. As you come across photos or articles that help make your vision more real to you, clip them out and paste them in your notebook.

A Day in the Life journal for a professional or service business might be structured like this:

- You are approaching your business from the street:
  o Where did you park?
  o How far did you have to walk?
  o Do you enter your business from the street or is it in an office building?
  o What does the front of your business look like?
    ▪ What are the colors and textures?
    ▪ What do you see in the windows?
    ▪ If it's in an office building, what does the lobby floors and walls look like?
    ▪ Is there an elevator? What is it like?
  o What is the hallway to your office like? Is there carpet, tile or marble on the floor?
  o How do you feel when you approach your business?

- You are at the threshold of your business
  - What is the first thing you see when you enter?
  - Panning from left to right, what does the interior look like?
  - What smells greet you?
  - What are the sounds inside the space?

- As you enter the space, focus on the experience you want your customers to have. ***Pretend you are the customer***.

For a Service Business:

  - How are you greeted? What is said? Who says it?
  - If you have to wait, is there a place to sit? Are there magazines or other amusements? What is the furniture like?
- When you are taken to where the service is delivered
  - What does this space look like?
  - What are the sounds and smells of this space?
  - Where do you stand or sit in this space?
  - When the person providing the service enters
    - How do they greet you?
    - What questions are asked?
    - How do you feel?
- Once you have received the service
  - Are you up-sold? What words are said?
  - How are you asked to make payment?
  - What is the transaction like?
    - Is it quick?
    - Are you billed later on terms?
    - Do you pay by cash, check or credit card?
  - How are you bid farewell? Who does it? What is said?
- You are leaving the business
  - How do you feel about the experience?

For a Retail Business:

- o Are you greeted? What is said? Who says it? How does it make you feel?
- You look for the item you wish to purchase on the sales floor
  - o What does this space look like?
  - o What are the sounds and smells of this space?
  - o How are the aisles/displays organized? Are they interesting? Exciting?
  - o Does the staff interact with you?
    - How are you greeted?
    - What questions are you asked?
    - How do you feel?
  - o Is it easy to find what you're looking for?
    - How are items categorized?
    - How is the store laid out?
    - Are prices clearly marked?
- After you have received the service
  - o What is the checkout process like?
    - Is it quick?
    - Is payment taken by the service provider or do you see a cashier?
  - o How are you bid farewell? Who does it? What do they say?
- You are leaving the business
  - o How do you feel about the experience?

These are just two examples of how you can create this *Day in the Life* journal. The limits are your imagination. What we've learned is when our clients have a clear idea of what their business is going to look, sound, feel and smell like, the closer they come to making it a reality. They have a model against which they can make adjustments. Many of our clients have walked through their business using the above outline from the viewpoint of their customers, even going as far as introducing problems into the experience so they can practice how to recover from them.

The value of this concept is enormous when it comes time to plan, start and run your business, because you will have answered the most difficult questions before they arise.

Step 2: Imagine Success

This is key: If you imagine your business as a quiet, empty place, that's what you will get. Actively visualize your business packed with excited customers. Hear the things they say and how you or your employees respond to them. Hear the cash register ring, the sound of a credit card being swiped. See and hear your customers enjoying the experience.

If you imagine nothing, then anything can fill that space, including fear, visions of failure and doubt. Your success vision is a defense against *FUD*, fear, uncertainty and doubt.

It's critical that you have concrete vision of success that is bigger than a giant stack of $100 bills. Immerse yourself in this success vision. Practice it and see it in your mind clearly and you will have a much greater chance of achieving it.

Step 3: Plan

As your *Day in the Life* journal takes shape, many elements of your business will get decided. Start capturing those elements in a chapter of your notebook that is separate from the information you are collecting for your business plan.

KEEP VISUALIZING As you get closer to realizing your idea, take steps to make it concrete. Some will have renderings done to get a sense of what the completed business will look like. You may even have a model made, but keep detailing your vision until you can see every time you close your eyes. Effortlessly, images of your idea will fill your mind, helping you rehearse your success.

All of the items you imagined and wrote in your journal will translate directly into the furniture and fixtures you will have in your business. It will tell you how many employees you will have and how they will look and act. The more detail you put into the visualization, the easier everything else will be.

Step 4: Discipline

Drummer Bill Bruford once said, *"The reason for discipline is the pursuit of accidents."* Your situation will change as you realize your vision. The economy will improve or deteriorate. The product you wish to sell will fall out of favor. Any of a host of things can occur that will impact your vision. That is why it's important to get the discipline of writing your journal and visualizing your success.

Once you have practiced this approach, you will have the ability to adjust your vision to match real world situations. You will be able to respond to incidents that change your course without becoming frustrated or giving up.

After you have created a clear picture of what your business will look like, set the goals that lead up to it:

End Goal:
A statement of what you want your business to be at the end of one year of operations, two years of operations, all the way to five years of operations.

Products and/or Services:

A statement of what you will sell (a product or service), its price points and how much it will cost you to purchase, create and deliver.

Opening Day State: What your business will look like, in detail, on opening day.

Location: Where will it be located and what will the building look like?
Furnishings and Fixtures: A preliminary list
Layout: A simple sketch
Hours of Operation
Employees: A list of jobs and the number of people required.

This document will become the basis of the initial planning for your business.

Chapter 7 - Who Is My Customer?

The Goal of This Chapter

Understand why customer identification is critical to success.

What You Will Do in This Chapter

Learn how to identify the customers you want to attract.

What You Will Have When You're Done

A good idea of who your customer is, how to reach them, how to attract them

Your customer will buy from you if you have what they want, presented in a way that appeals to them at a price they are willing to pay, in a location convenient to them.

As part of your visioning process, you need to begin thinking about the customers you want to attract to your business. Many people believe that 'anyone' can and will use their service or purchase their product, but in reality, you will have to make specific appeals to different groups of people. The greater your understanding of the groups you're targeting your message towards, the more successful you'll be.

While we cover the subject in depth in Part 3 where you develop your actual business plan, it's never too soon to start thinking about who your customers will be.

As part of your visualization process, we asked you to think about your business filled with excited customers. We asked you to think about what they looked and sounded like, imagining how they responded to the experience of doing business with you.

Now we want to take that a step further. We want you to look at the thing you're selling and your image of the customers who will buy from you and begin theorizing about who they are in depth.

In your visioning notebook, create a separate section called 'Customers'. Make sure to leave a block of pages so your observations can grow. In this section, start making some assumptions about your customers starting with the following attributes:

- Income
- Age
- Race
- Homeowners or Renters
- Location
- Employment
- Education
- Leisure Activities
- Television Preferences
- Radio Preferences
- Internet Use
- Travel
- Number of children/grandchildren
- ...

The list above contains a number of pieces of information. Some are called demographics which ask questions about items such as income, age or employment to build a picture of what the population looks like from an economic sense. Psychographics, or the questions about leisure and entertainment preferences, aims at getting a picture of how a specific population is thinking and feeling. Both sets of information are important to you.

Obviously, this is a lot to think about, but the more specific you make each type of customer; the better and easier it will be to attract them to your business.

One of the things that you'll find early on is that you don't have one single type of customer, but many types. It's also important to recognize that not everyone is your customer. Keep track of the attributes of individuals who will probably not buy from you as well.

How Location Affects Demographics/Psychographics

For most retail establishments in urban settings, about 85% of your customers will come from within one mile of your business, another 10% from a three mile radius and about 5% from within a five mile radius. This makes choosing a business location the most critical decision you will make. By considering the attributes of your customers, you will have an important window into that decision. People with the characteristics you're looking for should live within a five mile radius of your location.

The radius rule applies mostly to urban areas and has to be adjusted for other locales. For example, the suburban community that places nearly every residence two to three miles from arterial roads that lead to retail locations would have a larger radii based on the locations of competing shopping centers. Rural areas need to consider the wants and needs of the population within a very large area, since there is reduced competition.

The important thing to remember is once you've determined who will buy from you, you must find out where they live (or work) and locate your business convenient to them.

Service and professional businesses are affected differently. They can usually draw customers up to ten miles, depending on the novelty of their business. A physician or a lawyer will be able to draw from a larger radius because of the nature of the specialty they provide. If they have a lot of competition, then the radius rule will apply.

The key point is that you increase your odds for success if you position your business close to the people you believe will buy from it.

How Demographics/Psychographics Affects Your Location

No, we didn't just ask the same question a different way. What we mean is, how the attributes of your customers will affect your business space. Depending on whom you think your customer is, the following aspects of your business could be affected:

- Layout
- Decoration

66

- Furniture and Fixtures
- Environment
- Advertising
- Employee Selection
- Operating Procedures
- Methods of Payment and Payment Terms
- …

Really, just about everything is dictated by who you think your customer is going to be. That is why it deserves a lot of study, which we will do in Part 3. For now, we are going to work from the assumptions that you created from your vision of your business.

Use the outline from Chapter 6, "Visualizing Your Business" as a guide for your observations.

Spend several days working on this section, capturing your observations in your notebook.

Exercise 1

Find three businesses that do or sell something close to what you want to do. Go to those businesses and observe how they are outfitted, the way the employees interact with customers and how transactions are handled. Make a transaction yourself, if you can, to have a complete experience.

For professional services this may be a bit harder to do. Seek out those businesses that offer informational seminars or free initial consults to have the experience with those businesses.

In your notebook, make two columns + and − for each of the businesses and write down what you liked and didn't like about the business.

In addition, write down the appearance of the customers and your guess at how they fit in demographically. Were they mostly of a certain age group or gender? Were they wealthy or middle class? Were they at the location because of the love of a certain pastime or activity?

These observations, along with the visioning work you have done previously in this section will be invaluable when the time comes to plan your business in detail.

Exercise 2

Create a profile for three types of customers that you want to attract to your business.

Chapter 8 - Pulling It All Together

The Goal of This Chapter

Complete the Pulling It All Together document.

What You Will Do in This Chapter

After reading the instructions that follow, complete the Pulling It All Together document. The intention of this document is to make a record of the things you have decided about yourself and your business choice to refer to as you move toward launch day.

What You Will Have When You're Done

A completed Pulling It All Together document.

Pulling It All Together Document Instructions

1. List the aspects of your business 'Day In The Life' that were crystal clear to you. The elements of your vision that you can see clearly will be beacons to you as you move toward making your dream a reality. They will become the framework to which you add all of the information that you still need to learn or figure out.

2. What parts of your 'Day In The Life' were murky to you? These items are the ones you will focus on until they are crystal clear as well. Don't worry if the list is long, no one knows everything. After all, you're just getting started.

3. Does your business idea seem more or less risky to you now? Why or why not? Are you encouraged by what you've learned? Are you energized and positive about your idea? Do the risks seem more manageable now? If not, spend some time pondering why you feel that way.

4. Does the amount of effort required to start your business seem like something you can handle? Why or why not? This is probably the most important question in this document. You cannot open a business on sheer will, you must have passion for it. You will experience setbacks, delays and misfortunes of every conceivable kind. The trade is you will have successes that simply aren't possible in a career. In your mind, do the benefits outweigh the cost enough to put in the effort required?

5. Are the people you are targeting to be your customers, people that you like and would normally associate with? If not, will you be able to work with them? Explain. We cannot emphasize this enough. Know yourself and how you relate to others. Customers come in all colors, shapes and sizes with a thousand different beliefs and attitudes. To be successful, you must serve them, regardless of what they think or who they are. Every limitation you place on them is an impediment to your business. Enough limitations and you won't have one.

6. List the resources in your possession that you can use to start your business. (ex., financial, equipment, people, etc.) This is your starting point from a resource prospective and will be useful later on.

7. List the resources you must acquire to go forward. This list will also be useful later as you move toward launch day.

8. Which areas are you confident you can handle with no assistance? These are your core strengths in relationship to the business you're going to launch. These are the things you can do or have knowledge about or know how to find out about.

9. What areas will you need assistance with? List where you think you will need help from a professional, consultant or coach.

Once you have completed this part. Reread your answers and then put your work aside for a day or two to allow yourself some time to reflect.

You've taken inventory of your preferences and you've imagined what your business will look like. Now we'll pull all of this effort into focus.

For this part you will need your visioning notebook as we discuss some of the aspects of your choices. Feel free to refer to your work as you complete this section. This is not a test but a set of questions to help you get your bearings before committing to starting your business.

This form is also available at *www.killerbusinessplan.com*. See *'How to Use This Book'* for instructions on how to access it.

1. List the aspects of your business 'Day In The Life' that were crystal clear to you.

    _____

    _____

    _____

2. What parts of your 'Day In The Life' were murky to you?

    _____

    _____

    _____

3. Does your business idea seem more or less risky to you now? Why or why not?

    _____

    _____

    _____

4. Does the amount of effort required to start your business seem like something you can handle? Why or why not?

    _____

_____

_____

5. Are the people you are targeting to be your customers, people that you like and would normally associate with? If not, will you be able to work with them? Explain.

_____

_____

_____

6. List the resources in your possession that you can use to start your business.　(ex., financial, equipment, people, etc.)

_____

_____

_____

7. List the resources you must acquire to go forward.

_____

_____

_____

8. Which areas are you confident you can handle with no assistance?

_____

_____

_____

9.   What areas will you need assistance with?

_____

_____

_____

Once you have completed this part. Reread your answers and then put your work aside for a day or two to allow yourself some time to reflect.

Chapter 9 - Decision Document 2

The Goal of This Chapter

Complete Decision Document 2.

What You Will Do in This Chapter

After reading the instructions that follow, complete Decision Document 2. The intention of this document is to make a record of the things you have decided about yourself and your business choice to refer to as you move toward launch day.

What You Will Have When You're Done

A completed Decision Document.

Decision Document 2 Instructions

I am starting the following business: You should have narrowed your choice down to one option. The reason for this is that you will have some effort from this point working through the feasibility of your choice. In addition, you may find it difficult to have more than one focus without getting discouraged or confused.

I believe my customers will be: Write down all of the attributes of your customers, every detail you can think of. Use all of the information you have created to this point to come up with this description.

The areas I have a handle on are: List all of the aspects of starting your business that you believe you have in hand.

The areas I will need assistance with are: List all of the items you think you will need help with between here and launch day.

I think the next steps I need to take are: These are next steps on any front. It's important that you date when the step is due and then make your best efforts to complete the step by its due date.

Signature: You are creating a contract with yourself. When you sign on the line, you are committing to fulfill your obligations under it. It is a sacred trust . Don't take this lightly. You will become who you want to be when you honor the commitments you make to yourself.

This form is also available at *www.killerbusinessplan.com* by clicking on the 'Electronic Materials' item in the menu bar. See *"How to Use This Book"* for password instructions.

Decision Document 2

I am starting the following business:

_____
_____
_____

I believe my customers will be:

_____
_____
_____

The areas I have a handle on are:

_____
_____
_____

The areas I will need assistance with are:

_____
_____
_____

The next steps I need to take are:

Item _____ **Date** _____

_____
_____
_____
_____
_____

I affirm by my signature that these are my ideas and choices. I will accomplish the steps I have decided I need to take by the due dates I have specified.

Signature   **Date**

_____

Part 2 – How Much Money Will My Business Make?

Overview

The focus of this part is *feasibility*, that is, whether your business concept has a reasonable chance at success. At the conclusion of this part, you will have a good idea how much money your business will be able to make, where you will look for funding, whether your business is for-profit or non-profit and what kind of corporate structure you should consider for it. This information, taken with the decisions made in Part 1, will put you in the position to write a serious, workable business plan. The details of writing that business plan are laid out in Part 3.

The reason we stress this approach is because we have seen many people begin businesses they were on fire for, only to fold because of complexities and problems they could have foreseen. You wouldn't take a long distance trip without deciding the destination *and* making sure your car can make the trip *and* taking enough money or credit to pay your expenses. Because you've driven before, you know the laws, so you're not confounded by detours, speed limits and direction signs.

But those same people who would take that care on a road trip, launch businesses on hope and faith, without counting the cost or knowing if their vehicle can cover the distance. By completing this part, you will have greatly increased your chances that you *won't* be one of them.

The time to check your parachute is before you jump.

Part 2 Consists Of:

Chapter 10: Feasibility Model and Instructions. This Excel based model will provide a quick, rough order of magnitude estimate of how much you may be able to take home from your business idea.

Chapter 11: Funding sources are critical to start up as most businesses fail from under capitalization. This chapter deals with how you can find funding and what some of the qualifications are.

Chapter 12: This chapter discusses whether you should consider a non-profit business and some of the misconceptions surrounding them.

Chapter 13: Understanding your options regarding corporate structures is the focus of this chapter.

Chapter 14: This chapter formalizes the decision you've made in this part.

Chapter 10 - Feasibility Model and Instructions

The Goal of This Chapter

Select and complete the feasibility model appropriate for your business concept.

What You Will Do in This Chapter

Download and complete the model.

What You Will Have When You're Done

A reusable spreadsheet that will give a good idea of how much product or service you must sell to meet your goals.

Feasibility Model

The spreadsheet is a capacity calculation model designed to give you a high-level, rough estimate of the amount of money your business could make. This is a very important piece of information about your future business. If you think you only need to sell hundreds of items a month to make money, but you really need to sell thousands, it's best to have that information early on. If you are not going to make enough money to support the life style you desire, you will want to select a different product, adjust your business model, or choose a different business.

The profit numbers displayed in this section are before state and federal income taxes and do not take into account pay back of any loans or investment capital. They are a simple estimate of the operating profit of a business. We have included three models for your use, depending on the type of business you are going to start.

Model 1

This model is designed for those who are selling a service (i.e. financial planning), or are involved in creating the product they are selling (i.e. crocheted baby blankets). The calculations are based on how much time, (days per month and hours per day), you can commit to your business.

- Information needed:
    - Number of days you plan to work each month
    - Number of hours per day you are willing to work
    - The amount of time it takes to deliver your service or create your product
    - Number of people directly involved in delivering the service or creating the product
    - Retail price of the product

Model 1 available at *www.killerbusinessplan.com* by clicking on the 'Electronic Materials' item in the menu bar. See *"How to Use This Book"* for password instructions.

Model 2

This model is designed around total sales dollars for the year and the average revenue per sale. Expenses and cost-of-goods will be subtracted from this number to arrive at your profit before income tax.

- Information needed:
    - Gross sales dollars desired for the year
    - Average dollar amount of each sale
    - How much the product cost you (cost of goods)

Model 2 available at *www.killerbusinessplan.com* by clicking on the 'Electronic Materials' item in the menu bar. See *"How to Use This Book"* for password instructions.

Model 3

This model is useful for someone starting a retail business such as a restaurant or clothing store and is based on an estimated number of transactions and average revenue per transaction.

- Information needed:
    - o Estimated number of sale transactions for the year
    - o Expected average revenue per transaction
    - o Your cost for the product

Model 3 available at *www.killerbusinessplan.com* by clicking on the 'Electronic Materials' item in the menu bar. See *"How to Use This Book"* for password instructions.

Chapter 11 - Funding Sources

The Goal of This Chapter

Provide a basic understanding of the sources of funding available to most start up businesses.

What You Will Do in This Chapter

Read the Funding Sources material.

What You Will Have When You're Done

An idea of where you will raise money for your business idea.

Show Me The Money!

It's been over a decade since the movie *Jerry McGuire* made that line a catch phrase. It persists because it's true. When you're starting up, cash is king. For all but the simplest businesses, how much cash you can raise will determine the nature of your business (the size of the space you choose, your furnishings, etc.), or if you can start at all.

This is a very important point to consider. Before you've written your business plan or even pitched your business concept to anyone, you need to decide who to approach for the funding you need. In the first part, you made a brief inventory of the assets and resources you bring to the table. In this chapter, we will discuss the realities around funding your business.

Below is a discussion of the basic ways businesses are funded.

Bootstrapping or Self Funding

This comes from the old expression, *'Pull yourself up by your bootstraps'*, (which personally I've always had a hard time visualizing). The term means funding from your own resources and the revenue that comes in. It means that your product or service must be salable day one unless you have the resources to finance development. The good part is you don't need to ask anyone for money. The bad part is you don't get the money you didn't ask for. Plus, if your product or service doesn't sell, you'll lose the money that you put in.

Obviously this is a risky play, one that you must be certain will work since you are putting your resources at risk. It works well for businesses that are small enough that a failure isn't going to send you to bankruptcy court.

An unintended consequence of bootstrapping is you may trash your credit leaving you unable to get financing later. Measure twice, cut once. Many self funded companies run through the credit limits on their bank cards and start raiding their retirement accounts. This is not pretty to a banker.

Friends and Family

If you've looked at your situation and know that you will need more money or credit than you have personally, you can approach friends and family. We don't suggest you do that before you have a completed business plan but we do think you should consider if your friends and family have the resources to support your idea. Take a guess at how much you'll need and triple it. That is the money you'll need to raise.

The people you approach don't have to have cash. They can co-sign a loan or provide the collateral for you to get a loan yourself. They may be able to help you under a deferred payment arrangement or provide you access to suppliers at a discount. There are a million ways friends and family can help you, but cash will be an important one. Look at the amount you need to raise and then your list of potential investors. Do they have the resources to make your idea a reality? Even more importantly, will they actually risk *their assets for your dream*?

We cannot stress enough that you should have a good business plan to take with you when you pitch them. Not because they will need to see it, but because you need to go through the rigor of creating it. Creating a good business plan in advance is a sign of respect to your investors, and will go a long way toward building trust. Trust you will need if things don't go well. You don't want them to become your former friends and family. If you think we're being unreasonable with that statement, just imagine a 4th of July bar-b-que jammed with people whose money you've lost.

Bank

Banks can be a great source for start up capital. Once you've qualified, you'll receive your money and the bank will pretty much stay out of your way, *if you pay on time*. Performance on a bank loan builds your credit and makes it easier to raise money for expansion later.

To qualify for most bank loans, you need a FICO score of 650 or better, some kind of collateral that can cover the amount you are borrowing, generally offsetting 80 - 120% of the amount borrowed, depending on the bank. You will have to pass a character test. That means if you have a felony (like a DUI), a bankruptcy or an eviction, you will also have a hard time making your case. You will also need a cash infusion (money you are personally committing to the business) of 10 - 30% of the total amount borrowed. The bank will not fund you 100%. The thought is, if you are not willing to risk YOUR money, the bank isn't willing to risk THEIR money.

You will need a full business plan and pro forma cash flow projections to apply for a loan over $50,000 (sometimes even less) and most times you will be taken through the bank's Small Business Administration (SBA) department so the bank can get your loan guaranteed by the government, or in other words by you, the taxpayer. In that way, if you default on the loan, the bank will be able to recover most of the money it lent you.

This is an important distinction. The SBA only guarantees loans, it doesn't originate them. SBA rules are fairly flexible, but bank rules are less so and you will have to qualify under them.

85

Community Development Corporations

Community Development Corporations (CDC) are non-profit companies that find money, primarily for purchase of buildings or equipment, for small businesses and start-ups. They are specialty firms that exist only to make these kinds of deals and as such, have access to information about government assistance available to business owners. Most have their own funds, granted to them by the SBA and/or state and county governments, but they nearly always have to collaborate with a bank to get a deal done.

The reason they focus on tangible things like buildings and machinery is, that most times, these things can help you meet the collateral requirements. Sadly, caveat No.1 applies.

Retirement Accounts

Raiding

A lot of people look at the money in their 401k (or 201k, after 2008) and see the capital they need to get started. While this is tempting, stop for a minute and think about what you're doing. Retirement money is some of the most expensive you can get and the hardest to replace. You will pay a penalty of 10% plus the proceeds get thrown into regular income in whatever taxable year you pull it out. This usually results in a big tax bill. But more importantly, you are betting the money that took *years* to raise that you will be successful. If you can do this with no problem, then you are very confident or foolish. Most people will think twice about doing it because the risk is large.

86

Rollover Funding

Recently, several companies have emerged in this space such as BeneTrends and Guidant that allow you to roll over your 401K into shares of a 'C' corporation to fund your company. There are a lot of compliance rules around this structure, but in the current financial environment, it may be the only way to go. The same risks stated in 'raiding' apply to this kind of funding.

Loans

Many retirement accounts will allow you to borrow against them, some up to 80% of the amount you have in them. Most of these loans have small or no interest payments and the fees are usually low. You will likely have a repayment period and there can be penalties for failure to repay the funds.

Investors

Once someone asked Gandhi what he thought about western civilization. He replied, "It sounds like a good idea." The same may be said for investors. Another thing can also be said, "My momma told me, 'better shop around'". Before they revoke my poetic license, let me tell you what I mean.

Investors can bring more than cash. They can open doors and find you customers. They can introduce you to the powerful and influential in politics and business. They can get you the front page on a major trade magazine or show you the back door to boutique financing. They can do all that and more for a mere 5 to 10 times (some would say up to *30* times) return on their investment and large chunk of your company, *if they are what you think they are.*

Investors come in all shapes and sizes. Some know what they're doing, some don't have a clue. Some earned their money building companies, some got lucky while riding in the back seat of a successful deal. The problem for you is, as a novice, you may be too wowed or too shy to ask all the questions you should to know who they are before signing up with them. Whether or not they are a mentoring beacon guiding you to success or a pain inflicted on you between their rounds of golf is totally up to you, because you chose them.

We cover more about investors in Part 3, but for now, let's give you some basics:

- They usually only invest in things that will bring them, on paper, at least 5 to 10x or greater (some will suggest up to 30x for very early stage companies) return, unless you have a personal relationship with them.

- They are generally interested in cutting edge technology or innovative ideas. Usually, only people who launder money will invest $500K in a yogurt shop (it sounds funny, but it's actually true).

- Most of the time they will not be heavily involved in your company, so you will have to know what you're doing.

- Some will attempt to gain controlling interest in your firm, some will be more reasonable. Expect to trade 30% of your company, at minimum, for angel (initial) funding.

Money is usually raised in tranches (which literally means 'slices') by rounds. That means investors will give you money for a part of your launch, but usually not all. Early investors are called angels, because only an angel would invest in an early stage project. They will provide you with enough money, called seed money, to prove your business could work and shepherd you through the next rounds of funding. You will then go through additional rounds of funding (a, b, c, etc) until your company is self sufficient, is purchased or goes public. Then the investor picks up a check and moves on to work with a new start up.

Caveat No.2
Many investors want to see your business operating, not just on paper, before they give you money. That assures them there is real interest in your product or service and you have some idea how to run a business.

Grants

Grants are funds donated by the government, corporations or private individuals (foundations) to address specific issues. Government grants have *'public policy objectives'*, meaning the Congressman or agency that created the grant did so because they wanted people in the private sector to work in a specific problem area. For example, I saw a grant looking for someone to start *any* kind of public museum in the 9th ward of New Orleans after Hurricane Katrina. Most government grants will have a tightly focused objective similar to that.

Grants were created to provide funding so people could work on endeavors that won't usually be done as a commercial venture. This is an important thing to note. The likelihood of obtaining a grant to start a clothing store, construction company or dog kennel is near zero, because the marketplace already supports that kind of business and has an established method of funding it. If, on the other hand, you want to bring foot powered water pumps to sub-Saharan Africa for free, you can probably find a grant for that.

There are Small Business Innovation Research grants (SBIR) that are given to fund research into promising new technologies. In addition, each branch of the military grants hundreds of millions of dollars to companies to develop force protection and other technologies. Frequently these grants are given to for-profit companies. If you can qualify for them, you probably already know about them.

Corporate grants are generally looking to extend some part of the company's research and development by funding private firms to work on specific research and then claim rights to the results. These grants can be generous, but they can also result in your life's work becoming the property of the corporation that funded the grant. Some corporations have general business grants, but they are usually targeted to specific populations in specific regions. Some portion of these grants are available to for-profit companies.

Foundation grants can be found for nearly every area of endeavor and they are highly competitive. Usually the foundation will focus on the discipline that created it. Others, like the Pew Charitable Trusts, will provide grants in a number of fields.

These are the major ways you can raise money for your business. You may use one, or a combination of several, to get your business started. At this point you should have enough information to make an early guess regarding where your start up capital will come from.

Chapter 12 - Non-Profits

The Goal of This Chapter

Understand how non-profits and grants work together

What You Will Do in This Chapter

Learn the phases of non-profits and how donors and grants can compliment operations

What You Will Have When You're Done

A good idea of how non-profits work

A good idea of how grants work

Non-Profits

Non profit organizations are a gift to all of us. They serve the poor, bring education to impoverished areas, and enable people to worship the religion of their choice. They get shoes on kid's feet, meals to the elderly and legal assistance to the destitute. These are businesses that are run by people with a calling. Individuals who start a business for the benefit of others are special people.

To run such a business, one must have a strong sense of mission. The road to obtaining funding and delivering the services afterwards can be difficult but rewarding. Some of what follows may sound negative, but it's the reality of non-profits. If you are the person who wants to serve through a non-profit, take the following discussion as a preview of the process.

Note that if your business is usually one that is operated for profit, doesn't benefit anyone besides you (your customers don't count) and can't be linked to a public policy objective or a cause, it's highly unlikely that that you will receive grant funding, regardless of what people may tell you. A non-profit has to help someone to better themselves, move a public policy objective toward reality (fighting global warming or the idea of global warming) or do a job that needs to be done but can't be done by a for profit business (tearing down abandoned houses). You may find grants for for-profit companies that are working on issues such as health care and green technologies, but the point is you won't get a grant for opening a sandwich shop or an auto detailing business.

Let's get the profit part out of the way first. A for profit business means that you sell things for more than they cost you. You run your business, choose your market and products and for the most part don't have a lot of restrictions on how you do business. Most importantly, all of the profit you make is yours (and Uncle Sam's).

Non-profits are different. Let's start with the profit part first. You don't get to have one. Any excess earnings get plowed into a reserve or allocated to projects, but it doesn't go to you. You can collect a salary (which is monitored) and in rare instances, bonuses, but that's it. You are an employee of the company you own from a profit perspective.

What about all these people you hear about that are living lives of luxury as the heads of non-profit organizations? You hear about them at two different times; when they are at the height of their fund raising glory and when they are indicted. Most people don't get away with living lavishly at the top of a non-profit for long. You can receive a substantial salary running a large non-profit but you will almost never match the pay you can make in a for profit organization of the same size.

If you are not profit motivated, then what you want to do has to fit into what the government or private foundations are funding. This requires research. Lots of it. Government funding is tied to programs that are championed by politicians. Every election your source of funding is dependent on who wins the election. Private funding is at the choice of the boards of corporations or wealthy individuals that have their own agendas. Their largess is based on profits, so you are dependent on their performance, the make up of their board and the economy.

Your business plan has to be even better than a for profit organization because it has two distinct phases: Launch and Sustaining. Because of the capricious nature of charitable and grant funding, you must plan to be self-sustaining as quickly as possible. The best possible plan is one that has the business generating surplus revenue that can be held in reserve against dips in external funding.

Launch Phase

In the launch phase, you will be completing grant applications to public and private sources. While these are not structured like business plans, they contain nearly all the same elements, organized in the format the funding organization wants to see. For this reason, we strongly suggest that you complete a full business plan so you can lift the completed sections for use in your grant applications. We say applications because the competition for most grant money is fierce and you will likely have to go to multiple sources to acquire sufficient funding.

If you are seeking donations from individuals, you will more likely be successful if you know them personally or move in the same circles they do. Breaking into a group of wealthy donors from the outside is a difficult move to pull off. There are professional fund raisers you can work with, but they charge fees for their work and they can't guarantee a result.

Be careful when hiring grant writers. We have met some fabulous, ethical individuals in this field. Finding the right one can make your efforts much easier. Find the wrong one and you'll spend a lot of time and money and end up frustrated.

We have seen people with the mistaken belief (encouraged by unethical grant writers) that they could get grants to start restaurants, clothing stores and hair salons. None of them even got a response from any funding source, much less money. Be especially aware of internet based grant search firms. One client came to us after a grant writer submitted a funding request for her personal services business to a foundation interested in rebuilding a museum in the wake of hurricane Katrina. The company told her that they would continue their search for an extended period for free if funding wasn't found. They found and applied to four targets that were not even a close match in one year. When they searched for free they didn't present our client with a single target.

Most grant applications require you to discuss how you are going to make your organization self sustaining. Most multi year grants have declining disbursements to incent you to raise capital from other sources. This means you will have to seek out new grants or develop fund raising programs to fill the gaps as the grants decline.

Sustaining

Once running, you will have to quickly establish a group of donors, a fund raising strategy or source of new grant funding, or maybe all of them, to sustain your organization. You may hit a home run and receive perpetual funding from a public or private foundation but this generally only happens after you have proven your organization's efficacy. Until then you'll be fund raising continuously.

Regardless of the difficulties in securing funding, non-profits are still a very necessary part of our society. Our advice to those wishing to start one is to associate with the directors of as many non-profit organizations as you can. In fact, you might think about working in these organizations so you can learn the ropes.

Chapter 13 - Corporate Structures

The Goal of This Chapter

Understand the various legal ways you can set up your business.

What You Will Do in This Chapter

At a high level learn the advantages and disadvantages of partnerships, corporations, LLC's and sole proprietorships.

Understand the benefits and limitations of the different forms of business entities

What You Will Have When You're Done

A high level understanding of the different business entities

An idea of which business entity will fit your new business

Business Entities

The term business entity refers to the legal identity of your business. You can choose to run your business as a sole proprietor or you can choose to make your business a separate, legal person through a limited liability company (LLC), a partnership or an 'S' or 'C' corporation. As its own person, your corporation can enter into contracts, hold bank accounts, make investments, apply for loans or do just about anything a real person can do. Your company, as a separate legal person, can limit your personal liability if it's sued.

There is one limitation that applies to LLCs, partnerships and corporations: After you establish one of these entities, you can have no personal transactions through the business or comingling of funds or debt such as the business writing checks to pay your personal bills. If you do, your corporation can be treated as an 'alter ego', which means that, for legal purposes, it is not a separate entity, but another form of you. Considering the expense and effort required to establish a separate legal entity, it's a good idea to maintain this discipline.

The requirements for business entities vary from state to state, so you will need to research the requirements for your locale.

Sole Proprietor

Ownership
You (and your spouse, if working together or in a community property state) own the business.

Start Up
In most locales, starting a sole proprietorship is a matter of purchasing a business license and filing a fictitious name statement in a local newspaper to let people know what name you will be 'doing business as' (dba).

Operations
You manage all operations. If you hire people to work for you, you are still responsible for their actions.

Funding
You usually fund a sole proprietorship through your own assets or through loans or promissory notes. You can also have investors in a sole proprietorship. If you want to take money from investors, you will have to execute a promissory note to receive the funds, as you will not be able to issue shares of stock in your business.

Taxes
You will pay taxes on your income at the personal rate but you can use business deductions to reduce your tax burden.

Legal Liability
You have unlimited personal liability, meaning if your business is being sued, you are being sued. Your personal assets, up to and including your home, car and bank accounts would be at risk.

Advantages
The advantage to being a sole proprietor is that it's the easiest and least expensive way to get into business. If you carry the correct insurance coverage, you can limit your legal exposure to acceptable levels.

Disadvantages

A disadvantage of a sole proprietorship is that you cannot easily take on investors or transfer a percentage of ownership in the business for funding. Another disadvantage is if your insurance doesn't cover a claim, or that claim is beyond the insurance policy cap, then your personal assets are at risk.

Partnership (non-corporate)

Ownership
There are two types of partners possible: general partners and managing partners. The distinction between the types will be made below. You may have an unlimited number of general partners. Ownership between the partners is usually determined by the amount of capital (money, assets and/or intangibles such as potential deals) contributed by each partner.

Partners, subject to some limitations, and depending on how the partnership is structured are able to transfer ownership of their interest in the partnership.

Start Up
To start a partnership, you will draft a partnership agreement (requirements vary from state to state) that details the contributions, rights and obligations of each partner. You will also have to register your partnership with the state. Each state has different filing requirements, so additional documents may be required.

Operations
The business will be operated as provided for in the partnership agreement, with each partner having the same authority to commit the business if all are general partners. The partnership can choose a managing partner to direct operations. In that case, only the managing partner has authority to legally obligate the business.

Funding
Funding can only be raised in cash or through loans or promissory notes. There are no shares of stock to sell to investors outside the partnership.

Taxes
The partnership itself pays no taxes. All tax liability flows through the partnership, to each partner where they are taxed, on the basis of their share of the business, at a personal rate.

Legal Liability
General partners have unlimited personal liability for debts and legal judgments incurred by the partnership.

Advantages
A partnership is a good way to get multiple people involved in starting a business. 'Flow through' taxation reduces the tax burden.

Disadvantages
The primary disadvantage of a partnership is unlimited legal liability along with the inability to raise investment capital. In the case of litigation your assets, like a sole proprietorship, are on the line directly.

Limited Liability Company (LLC)

Ownership
Owners of LLCs are called member(s). There are two types of members, members and managing members.

There is no limitation on the number of people who can be part of an LLC and there are no restrictions on citizenship of the member(s). Ownership in an LLC is freely transferrable, if the operating agreement allows it.

Start Up
An LLC has two main components. The first is the Articles of Formation, which describes what the LLC will be in business to do and who the members are. The second is the Operating Agreement, which describes how the business will operate and what members have authority to take what actions.

In addition, the operating agreement will spell out how distributions are made from the company, how members may sell or transfer their ownership interest and what steps must be taken to dissolve the LLC.

Operations

LLCs are operated by all member(s) unless they elect managing member(s). In that case, the managing members will operate the business and the members have no say in the day to day operations.

No annual meetings are required and no paperwork documenting major business decisions is needed, unless specified by the operating agreement.

Funding

LLCs are generally funded by the member(s) contributing something of value for a percentage of ownership.

LLCs may, in some states, issue shares of stock to member(s) and there can be different classes of stock (common, preferred, non-voting, founders). If an LLC is going to use stock to raise capital from outside investors, those outside investors will become member(s) of the LLC and therefore subject to the taxation features of it. There are also significant SEC requirements that must be met for outside investors.

Taxes

LLCs have 'flow through' taxation, meaning the LLC itself does not pay taxes, but each member pays at the personal rate for their share of earnings. You can elect to have your LLC treated as a "C" corporation for tax purposes, see "C" corporation for details on how it is treated for tax purposes.

Legal Liability

LLCs provide limited liability against debtors, shielding member'(s) personal assets should the entity be sued. The liability to the LLC is for amounts invested or loaned to it, unless the member(s) have personally guaranteed repayment of funds. In that case, they will be personally liable for repayment as if they made the note themselves.

LLCs also provide some protection from errors and omissions and/or general liability. This protection is not a substitute for proper insurance.

It is important that the business of the LLC and personal business be kept completely separate. In litigation, if the plaintiff can prove commingling of funds, the LLC can be invalidated, eliminating the protections it provides.

Advantages
Compared to corporations, an LLC is simpler to set up and maintain. No board of directors is required. There is no annual meeting required and major decisions do not have to be documented, although it's a good idea if you do. Flow through taxation lowers your tax burden, as compared to a "C" corporation.

Disadvantages
Some states have limitations on LLCs and how they operate. Using stock to raise capital is cumbersome.

In some states, such as California, LLCs are subject to gross receipts tax that makes them more expensive to operate than S corporations as taxable income grows.

S Corporation

Ownership
Partners own S corporations. There are two types of partners, managing partners and general partners.

Start Up

To start an S corporation, you will need to create and file 'Articles of Incorporation'. This document describes the business purpose, capital structure and operations of the business.

Operations
If there are no managing partners, the any general partner can obligate the company by committing purchase orders and/or contracts. If there are managing partners, only they can legally commit the company. If they are in place, the general partners are indemnified against any liability for the actions of the managing partner.

S Corporations have board meetings, usually no less than every quarter and you are required to have an annual shareholders meeting where you report on the state of the business.

Funding

The capital of an S corporation is contributed by the partners of company. Usually the percentage of ownership is determined by the amount of capital contributed by each partner.

Taxes

S corporations have 'flow through' taxation, meaning the company itself does not pay taxes, but each shareholder pays at the personal rate for their share of earnings.

Legal Liability

S corporation partners are generally not liable for the debts of the company unless they personally guaranteed them. Shareholders are also generally not liable for the acts of a corporation unless they were a managing partner.

Partners are generally shielded from responsibility for the debts and legal acts of a corporation.

Advantages

The S corporation combines the partnership structure with the legal protections of a legal entity. Its lower tax rate makes it a favorable choice over an LLC while providing the same flow through tax treatment.

Disadvantages

S corporations have rigid reporting requirements as well as limits on the type of investor the company can have.

C Corporation

Ownership

Shareholders own C corporations. The stock they hold can be of different classes (common, preferred, founders) in different series (Series A will generally have different rights than Series B) and can be voting or non-voting. Generally, unless they are officers or employees of the company, they will have no role in the day to day operations of it.

Shareholders can transfer their shares to anyone as long as the Articles of Incorporation allow such sale. Some companies restrict the sale of stock.

Start Up
To start a C corporation, you will need to create and file 'Articles of Incorporation'. This document describes the business purpose, capital structure and operations of the business.

Operations
C Corporations are run by a board of directors who appoint officers (CEO, Controller, etc.) to run the day to day operations of the company. The directors and/or officers may or may not be share holders of the company although they generally are.

C Corporations have board meetings, usually no less than every quarter and you will have an annual shareholders meeting where you report on the state of the business.

This is an important point, if as owner, you elect to become a C corporation and appoint a board, technically, you have to go to that board for every major business decision, as detailed in your Articles of Incorporation. Those decisions must be documented in the minutes of each board meeting.

Funding
Start up capital is raised through the sale of stock. There are no restrictions on the number of classes or series of stock that you may offer.

Taxes
The income made by C corporations is taxed twice. First, the corporation is taxed at the corporate level, usually at a rate less than the personal rate. Then the dividends and/or salaries paid to the owners of the business are taxed at the personal rate. The only tax advantage is that the owners don't pay at the higher personal rate for funds not disbursed to them.

Legal Liability
C corporation shareholders are generally not liable for the debts of the company unless they personally guaranteed them. Shareholders are also

generally not liable for the acts of a corporation unless they are a director or officer in the company.

Directors and officers are generally shielded from responsibility for the debts of a corporation but not its acts, for which they can be held personally accountable. Further, directors and officers of C corporations have a fiduciary responsibility to shareholders, requiring that they act in the shareholders' best interest. Directors and officers of corporations can be sued in the event of under performance or failure of the company. They can also face criminal charges for the illegal acts of their company.

Advantages
A C corporation allows the raising of capital through the sale of stock, opening ownership to passive investors. The lack of restrictions on type of stock allows maximum flexibility in raising capital. This form offers legal and debt liability protection.

Disadvantages
C corporations require a board of directors, periodic meetings, an annual shareholders meeting and much more documentation than other business entities, except S corporations.

Owners of C corporations are taxed twice, once on the earnings of the company and again at the personal level on all disbursements.

Some important points

When you are starting out, you are likely to be required to personally guarantee a loan or lease you take, even if it is in the name of the corporation. This means from a practical point of view, you receive no protection from creditors by having a business entity. Because of that, some people start as a sole proprietor until they know that the business will be a success and then they incorporate. Be sure to carry appropriate liability insurance to cover any other legal threats.

If you must raise money from investors, you will need to create an LLC, S or C corporation. Be aware that SEC rules limit the number of investors that you may have (35 as of this writing, regardless of type of corporation) and they must be registered as "qualified investors" meaning they have experience investing directly in early stage companies and have the net worth (usually $1MM) to weather losing their investment. Also, you may not advertise to the public to draw potential investors.

Chapter 14 - Decision Document 3

The Goal of This Chapter

Complete Decision Document 3

What You Will Do in This Chapter

After reading the instructions that follow, complete the Decision Document. The intent of this document is to make a record of the initial decisions you've made regarding your business and its structure. Compare your responses to what you have written in the previous two decision documents to make sure they are consistent with each other. Make sure the decision documents become part of your planning notebook.

What You Will Have When You're Done

A completed Decision Document.

Decision Document Instructions
My business has the following performance characteristics:

Type of Business

Describe the type of business as specifically as possible. (ex: I am starting a women's boutique clothing store).

Launch Date

The date that you will be open for business. Make it realistic.

Revenue

What is the total amount of money the business will make each year.

Gross Profit

The amount of money you will have after deducting your cost-of-goods (COGS).

Net Profit

The amount of money you will make after all expenses are paid.

of Transactions

This is the number of sales of your product or service you need to reach your goals

of Employees

How many people will you need to work with you to reach your goals.

Type of Location

The type of space, home office, retail space or industrial space.

My business will be a for-profit or non-profit for the following reasons:

Will your business be for or not for profit? If you're selecting a non-profit business, what problem does it solve? Are there other companies doing what your business will do? What makes you different?

I will seek funding from these sources:

List the possible sources for money to start your business. If you are thinking about approaching multiple sources, list them in order of probability. List the pros and cons of each.

If I can't find funding at my primary sources, my fall back plan is:

If your primary sources don't work out, what will you do? It's important to consider this, since creating a business plan and seeking funding is a lot of work.

I will structure my business using this entity (sole proprietor, partnership, LLC, S corp, C corp):

What corporate structure will you use? If you plan to use different ones at certain times in your company's development, list them.

The next steps I need to take are:

List your next steps.

I have decided the following things about myself:

I am what I think I am

I can be whatever I choose to be

I can accept information contrary to the beliefs I have about myself

I can change any aspect of myself that is in conflict with who I want to be

_____

_____

_____

My business has the following performance characteristics:

Type of Business		Launch Date	
Revenue		Gross Profit	
Net Profit		# of Transactions	
# of Employees		Type of Location	

My business will be a for profit or non profit for the following reasons:

_____

_____

_____

I will seek funding from these sources:

_____

_____

_____

To seek funding, I will need:

_____

_____

_____

If I can't find funding at my primary sources, my fall back plan is:

_____

_____

_____

I will structure my business using this entity (sole proprietor, partnership, LLC, S Corp, C corp):

_____

_____

_____

I think the next steps I need to take are:

Item   Date
_____

_____

_____

_____

I affirm by my signature that these are my ideas and choices and that I will accomplish the steps I have decided I need to take by the due dates specified.

Signature   **Date**

_____

Part 3 – Building Your Business Plan

Overview

If you've completed the first two parts of this book, then you already know what your business will be, whether it's a start-up, purchase or franchise, who you're selling to and how much your business is likely to make. Now you're ready to take on writing the business plan. Because you've done this pre-work, the plan should be easier to create than had you just gotten an outline and dove in.

Throughout this part we will refer to three case studies; using them to illustrate the important points of each chapter.

 ***Gone to the Dogs*** is a dog day care and grooming business. This case is extensively documented and includes a complete set of videos to help you work the financial model.

 ***Astro Hydraulics*** is a manufacturer that produces parts for business jets.

 ***On your Side*** is a business coaching service

Our suggestion is that you follow a case study through the various chapters to see how to complete each part. We varied the types of businesses to provide you with a number of examples to follow.

We also include a number of pro forma cash flow financial templates for you to use. The one you pick is based on the number of revenue streams you have.

If you can see it, you can achieve it.

110

Part 3 Consists Of:

Chapter 15: Is an overview of the different reasons business plans are written, the layout of a business plan and the best way to go about creating one.

Chapter 16: Is an overview about how to design and describe the operations of your business and your products and services.

Chapter 17: Pro forma cash flow and instructions. In this chapter you will create a pro forma cash flow model for your business idea.

Chapter 18: This chapter discusses how to determine your NAICS code and how to conduct research on your industry.

Chapter 19: In this chapter you will identify and learn about your customer.

Chapter 20: This chapter discusses the different marketing techniques so you can create a marketing plan. A marketing plan is the key to making the public aware of your business and making your business a success.

Chapter 21: This chapter details the organizational plan of the business including the background of the principals and a description of the various positions in the organization.

Chapter 22: Is an overview on how to write an executive summary. The executive summary is your three-minute window of opportunity to grab the reader's attention.

Chapter 23: This chapter finalizes your business plan by putting it all together into a presentable document.

Chapter 15 - Business Plan Overview

The Goal of This Chapter

To learn:
The different reasons business plans are written
The layout of a business plan
The best way to go about creating one

What You Will Do in This Chapter

Read the business plan overview.

What You Will Have When You're Done

A good understanding of how you should approach writing your business plan, what you will need to include in it and what to expect while writing it.

Reasons to Write a Business Plan

The main reason you create a business plan is to know what your business will look like, what it will cost to operate and how much profit you can expect it to produce. Done correctly, the business plan will help you understand how to start your business. It will give you a good estimate of how much capital you need. Once in business, it will provide a way to measure your results, so you can get ahead of small problems before they become big ones. It will also help you to clarify the characteristics of the business so you can explain it to others.

Aside from those basic reasons, there are other purposes for a business plan. We discuss these reasons below, because they affect the content of the plan:

- **Raising Capital:** In Part 2 of this book you selected the means you will pursue to fund your business. If you are not self funded, then your business plan will be as much a sales document as it is an operational description. This does not mean that you will pile on flowery prose or gratuitous self promotion, but you will highlight the strengths of the management team and your product.

  - Plans seeking funding from banks will focus strongly on pro forma projections and the skills and experience of the management team. They will require a tightly reasoned marketing plan and a good understanding of the market. You will be judged as much on the clarity of your vision as you will on the amount of money your project will make.

    In addition, *character counts* hugely with banks, since liquidating your assets is the last thing they want to do. If you have a bankruptcy, foreclosure or charge off on your record you will have to have an excellent reason for it.

  - If you're talking to investors, depending on the nature of the business, your plan will look somewhat different.

    - For private investors funding traditional businesses, your plan will be more in line with what you will send to a bank, but you will need to provide an exit for the investor, which is discussed later.

    - Investors in a new concept or high technology business are less concerned with pro forma financials than they are with a market for your product. These are the investors that aren't bothered by the classic "hockey stick" revenue model, since they know it's difficult to project revenues for something new.

    - You must have a solid grasp on who you would sell to and why they would buy.

Investors will want to know the problem your product solves or what will make it compelling. Investors are usually less interested in products that make incremental improvements to existing products, than products that solve a new problem. They are also looking for your knowledge, ability and enthusiasm. The details of your business plan will vary depending on your stage in the product development cycle. For early stage companies, your plan could be as simple as a PowerPoint presentation. You should know as much as possible about the investors and their due diligence process so you can plan appropriately.

- **Operational:** An operational business plan is more internal to the business and is more focused on how things get done or how the organization is structured. Since the objective is to provide a clearer management picture, less effort is spent on featuring the things that banks or investors would ordinarily look for. Operational plans are usually written as part of a re-alignment or merging of two organizations or when a company has grown over time and wants to document its structure and operations and solidify its goals.

- **Expansion:** Expansion plans are created when a company is going to add significantly to its capacity, change or add to the products it sells or integrate an acquired business into itself. These plans are created so the participants will know what their targets are after the expansion and to keep them out of trouble while they are implementing it.

If the plan is part of an acquisition, it may be written prior to the acquisition of a target and revised to take into account the nature of the business being merged. Frequently these business plans become the basis for the due diligence effort.

A Good Business Plan Tells a Story

People like stories, that's why there are 500 channels on cable and new books are being published and movies released every week. The idea of telling stories to advance business concepts has become so popular that companies have sprung into existence to teach executives how to be story tellers.

Successful entrepreneurs understand the importance of developing a theme. The theme requires clear objectives since it is a short hand description of them. Clear objectives mean a better chance of success.

Themes to think about:

- Create a theme of uniqueness. Position your business, or the way customers can use your business, in a unique manner.

- Create a theme of service. Competent, well-trained sales clerks, delivery employees, repair technicians - anyone with customer contact must look and act as professionals.

- Create a theme of comfort and pleasure. Make your customers feel good about doing business with you. Pay attention to their well-being and the reason they are willing to spend their dollars on your products or services.

- Create a theme of value at a reasonable price.

It can be challenging to promote your business as having the most value at competitive prices, but is important to standout in the market.

Boiling your theme down to a tag line will help you stay focused on the overall message of the business plan.

Here are some tag lines of business your familiar with:

Home Depot

"You Can Build It. We Can Help"

Home improvement center - combined with knowledgeable sales help and "low" prices. A one-stop shopping experience for "do-it-yourself" homeowners based on savings and pride of accomplishment.

Nordstrom

"Customer service"

Fashion retailer - Customer service is its top priority. It wants the customers to feel special. Their marketing strategy is word of mouth from satisfied customers.

State Farm Insurance

"Like a Good Neighbor, State Farm is There"

Insurance Company- they want you to feel cared for by someone who knows you. There are promoting intimacy and trust.

Coca-Cola Company

"Open happiness "

Beverage manufacturer - equates their soft drink with happiness and fun.

Business Plan Sections and Definitions

There are many ways to structure a business plan. The outline that we provide for you has been used by our company to successfully fund hundreds of businesses in dozens of different industries. There are other templates out there and we invite you to examine them and borrow from them if you believe there is an advantage to you.

The format we discuss below has evolved over the course of years of practice. It strikes a balance between brevity and providing enough information to get the attention of someone who can write a check. Underwriters, the people who make the decision about bank funding, love our plans because they are complete but not repetitive or overwhelming.

	Section	**Where Discussed**
1.	Executive Summary	Chapter 22
2.	Financial Needs	Chapter 22
3.	Company Description	Chapter 16
a.	Vision	
b.	Mission	
c.	Goals	
4.	Operations	Chapter 16
5.	Fixed Plant and Assets	Chapter 16
6.	Market Analysis	
a.	Industry Description	Chapter 18
b.	Customer Attributes	Chapter 19
c.	Competitive Landscape	Chapter 20
7.	Product/Service Offering	Chapter 16
8.	Promotion	Chapter 20
a.	Goal	
b.	Strategy	
c.	Marketing Plan	
9.	Personnel	Chapter 21
10.	Principals	Chapter 21
11.	Financial Assumptions	Chapter 17
12.	Financial Models	Chapter 17

1. **Executive Summary** is to be placed at the front of your narrative, but is written *last* to ensure your summary accurately reflects your business plan.

2. **Financial Needs** can consist of a short sentence or paragraph clearly stating the loan amount you are seeking for your business, and what the money will be used for (e.g. Working capital, equipment). In some business plans this section is also called "Use of Funds." You can use either title.

3. **Company Description**

   a. *Vision* is a description of the business as you want it to be. In dictionary terms it is, "a mental image produced by the imagination." It involves seeing the optimal future for the business, and vividly describing this vision. The description should include what kind of contribution your business will make to its field or the community.

   b. *Mission* (or purpose) is what the business is going to do. It is likely to cover the customer groups that are being served, as well as (perhaps more importantly) the customer needs that are being met.

      Vision and Mission should:
      - Bring focus and clarity to the desired future of the business (and what makes it distinctive)
      - Inspire people to work towards that future
      - Guide people in their decision-making as they reach for this future
      - Provide customers with a sense of what the company is about

   c. *Goals.* A business may have a number of goals, each describing a desired future condition toward which effort is directed. The starting point in writing business goals is to ask, "How do we know we've accomplished our mission". For business plan purposes, this section reflects the business' financial goals.

      Financial projections will estimate the total revenue

and net income of the company's cash flow. These are the numbers reflected in your financial goals. Not all business plans include such projections if funds are not being immediately sought.

For those not seeking funding your goals will reflect the steps you are taking to realize your vision and mission, and how you will know you've achieved them.

4. **Operations** are activities involved in the running of your business including location, size and hours of business. Be sure to include a high-level description of day-to-day activities and procedures of the business.

    For your own benefit, all primary operations should be detailed down to the simplest process. Think about what steps are required to complete a transaction down to the basics of designing or ordering the product. Move onto internal operations, such as assembly, customer service, ordering or shipping (if applicable), etc. All processes and operations should be detailed so that you know exactly what you are going to do, and how you are going to do it. Don't focus on the specifics of the actual product or service, as that will be covered in a separate section. If you choose to include your processes, put them into an appendix to the plan. The more detail you provide the better the funding source will feel about your ability to run the business.

5. **Fixed Plant & Assets** are used in the operations of your business. Plant, machinery and equipment, furniture and fixtures, and tenant improvements comprise the fixed assets of most companies because they are depreciable. This section is generally comprised of a short list, but in the case of a manufacturing or distribution enterprise can run to several pages. If your equipment list is large, you may want to make it an appendix and refer to it from this section.

6. **Market Analysis** is an opportunity to share all relevant research you have gathered that supports the existence of your business. This section may be anywhere from 2-8 pages depending on size of the market. The market analysis consists

of three sections: (1) Industry Description, (2) Customer Attributes and (3) Competitive Landscape.

- o **Industry Description** is drawn from your previous market research (if you completed Parts 1 and 2) of the industry you are in. All information and statistics used in the plan must be chosen wisely to support the presence of your business in a growing lucrative industry. Bankers and investors want to see what kind of niche you can make for your business.

- o **Customer Attributes** describe the characteristics of your potential customers. Who they are. How much they make. Where they live. Anything that describes your customers, and why they will purchase your product/service.

- o **The Competitive Landscape** section first identifies your direct and indirect competitors and then introduces their offerings. If you have no direct competition, explain how prospective customers are likely to react to your offerings and relate your offerings to the nearest equivalent competitors or solutions. Highlight similarities and differences between your offerings and competitors' in terms of price, features, quality, availability, design, etc. Sometimes the best way to get information on your competition is by calling them as a "prospective customer" and getting a feel for what they do.

  Even if there are no competitors doing exactly what you do, you are always competing against the *status quo*. Going along with how things are is human nature. How will you get your customers to change their current behavior to include you in their lives?

7. **Product/Service Offering** generally devotes three/four paragraphs to explaining what your offering is and what you do. Explain where and how your products and services are used, and why customers need them and will buy them. *Minimize technical terms.*

8. **Promotion** is the section of the narrative consisting of three topics: Goals, Strategy, and Marketing Plan.

    o   The **Goal** is a statement that clearly describes the target you are shooting for, usually expressed in market share and or gross revenue.

    o   **Strategy** is where you define your plan for gaining customers. Mentioning how you plan to segment the market is also helpful. The purpose of segmenting a market is to allow you to focus on the consumers "most likely" to purchase your offering. If done properly this will help to insure the highest return for your marketing/sales dollars.

    o   The **Marketing Plan** consists of an advertising and promotional plan and the tactics you will use. Often this refers to ways in which you will make your business known to the public. This could include media, such as newspapers and mailings, or networking at local functions such as a Chamber of Commerce or a local charitable or fine arts related function.

9. **Personnel** refers to a short list of all employee titles, duties, and the number you will be employing. Below each title you may include a short list of job descriptions.

    o   Some funding sources also like it if you include an additional section about the company organization if there are various levels of authority. A flowchart or organization chart can be used to explain who reports to whom, and how the company will be run.

10. **The Principals** section includes a paragraph for each principal or officer of the business. A principal is usually an owner of the enterprise, but can be a manager or other key person who is largely responsible for business operations.

11. **Financial Assumptions** are used to explain your cash flow model, if you intend to include one in your plan. You must

provide an explanation for the numbers chosen, inflation rates, boosts or declines in specific revenue streams, etc. The more detailed your assumptions are, the fewer questions you deal with later.

12. **Financial pro-forma cash flow and break-even models.** We provide you with templates that you can use to build your models.

The pro forma financial models are available at *www.killerbusinessplan.com* by clicking on the 'Electronic Materials' item in the menu bar. See *"How to Use This Book"* for password instructions.

How Long Should My Business Plan Be?

There's no "right" length for a business plan; it should be long enough to give the type of detail that is needed to lay out your plans in a clear and concise way, without wandering down unnecessary paths. Depending on the complexity of the business, generally plans are no longer than 20-40 pages. One way to make sure that your plan is as concise as possible is not to repeat any information unless absolutely necessary. If you do repeat information, be sure not to use the exact same words but paraphrase or rewrite, summarize, or give more detail to allow a deeper or different understanding of the information.

This is an important point. There is a difference between detail and density. Detail adds to reader understanding. Density is repeated information or the addition of non-relevant information to "bulk up" a plan. People who read through business plans for a living know the difference. *Don't waste their time!*

Images and Graphs

One way to enhance any narrative is to include relevant pictures, graphs, maps and statistics. Not only does the use of these images help clarify specific points, but also they make the business plan more aesthetically pleasing and less of a grind to read. Images often give a better explanation of your product/service, competitive landscape and industry research than just words.

Pictures of your product or business location will do much to make your case with the bank and reinforce your narrative. If you are unable to include photos of your actual product or location, pictures may be found on any search engine that allows for an image search, such as Google Images or Yahoo Images. By typing in keywords, relevant photos may be saved to your computer and used in the narrative.

Disclaimer: Use pictures sparingly to enhance understanding and make a point. Only use relevant images.

For purposes of example, we will be using the highlights of three business plans at the same time. The purpose is two fold, to give you examples that you can draw some insights from when writing your own plan and to show you that there is no 'one' way to write a plan. The most important thing is that the plan is as specific to your business idea as possible and that it's easy to understand. The three businesses we'll be using are quite different from each other, but each has information that can be used in any business plan:

Gone to the Dogs

Gone to the Dogs is a dog grooming salon with day care that also has a staff that performs in house visits to feed and walk pets left at home.

(Service and merchandising business with four revenue streams with three streams requiring cost of goods calculation).

Astro Hydraulics

Astro Hydraulics is a firm that manufactures a landing gear component for small jets. *(Manufacturing operation with six revenue streams requiring cost of goods calculation for each line).*

On Your Side

On Your Side is a solo business coach working out of a home office.

(Sole proprietorship with a simple two stream cash flow with no cost of goods calculation).

While one of these models may be more applicable to your situation than another, we suggest that you take a look at each one of them since there may be parts of each that you want to combine to create your plan.

Business Plan Writing Strategy

It's a good idea to look at what you're good at, as well as pinpointing the places you'll get stuck, before starting a project like writing a business plan. There are three main skills you need to complete your plan:

> • **Access to research and the willingness do it** – Your plan will be as good as the facts you base it on. Work to get the most recent and relevant information you can find. This is the most important part of the plan where you find out what's going on in the field you want to be in. For most people it will also take the most time. It's best that you do most of the research yourself, or at least take an active part in creating it, so you are well grounded in the information.

> *What to do if this is not a strong area for you*: You can seek out the help of friends and family. You can also approach non-profits, such as SCORE, or small business development centers (SBDCs) for assistance, but they will not do the research for you, they will provide you with guidance. You can also hire a business consultant to perform the research for you. If you do hire a consultant, pick one that will keep you involved with the research process and not just hand off a finished product to you. You really need to know what's going on first hand.

> • **Reasonable writing skills** – You don't need the prose of a best selling author to communicate your business idea. You do need to be able to construct logical sentences and paragraphs.

> *What to do if this is not a strong area for you*: Of the three areas, this is probably the easiest to compensate for. You can work with a friend or relative to write the plan. You can also contact the business department of many colleges that have intern programs and arrange for an intern to assist you with writing the plan. You can also work with SCORE, SBDC or other non-profits. Or you can hire a professional writer or business consultant that focuses on writing plans.

- **Discipline** – Writing a business plan is not a one day job or a weekend project. To write a good business plan you should plan on spending an extended period of time, or many smaller blocks of time. As professionals with hundreds of plans under our belt, we can do a plan in about 7 to 10 working days. You should plan to spend a concentrated effort over one to two months, or more, to complete your plan. Some people find that working on the plan every day for an hour produces the best results, others find that spending more time less frequently works for them. Do what works for you, but establish a pattern and stick to it.

What to do if this is not a strong area for you: This will be tough to overcome. If you cannot muster the discipline to get your business plan done, imagine what it will be like in your business where you will have to get the job done, regardless of whatever else is happening in your life. We all have life occurrences and inconveniences that set us back, but if you can't find the time to formulate a plan, you need to reconsider whether you should start a business at all.

Having said this, there are those who are disciplined, but just have too much going on to dig as deep as needed to put together a good plan or they recognize that research and writing are not strong suits for them. To those individuals we recommend working with a professional business plan writing service. But beware of any service that tells you it can write a business plan based on a single interview or a questionnaire. Choose a firm that uses a workshop based or iterative approach to writing your plan. Most importantly, make sure that the plan they sell you has all the appropriate sections completed in sufficient detail. Finally, make sure you are included in the process. After all you are the one who will be taking the risks.

As you begin writing your business plan, resist the urge to write the sections serially, that is one section after another. If you use this method, you will try to complete each section only to find that the specifics of your plan keep changing, meaning you will have to keep editing prior sections. A better approach is to include information in the appropriate section when you gather it. This way the plan will start to finish itself as you do your research and make decisions about your business model.

You will notice that we take the sections in the order of importance that makes sense to us. For example, you have to figure out how your business will function before you can build financials. You should do the financials to know if it's worth completing the plan. By using a progressive method, the impacts of changes are greatly lessened.

Don't worry about grammar or how things fit together at first, that's what you will catch on your *many* re-reads of the plan. Just get the words on paper.

Chapter 16 - Operational Design

The Goal of This Chapter

Learn the definition of Vision, Mission and Goals
Learn how to design and describe the operations of your business.
Learn how to describe the products and services of your business.

What You Will Do in This Chapter

Write a draft of your Vision and Mission and define high level achievable goals
Design and describe the operations of your business
Describe your products and services in more detail

What You Will Have When You're Done

An understanding of Vision and Mission and how they relate
An understanding of why goals are important to a company
An understanding of what operational design is and why it is important
The content for your operations section
Basic parameters for your pro forma financial model
Product and services write up

Vision/Mission/Goals

Vision and Mission Statements should clearly and concisely communicate the direction of the company and its purpose for existing. Together they should:

- Bring focus and clarity to the desired future of the business (and what makes it unique)
- Inspire people to work towards that future
- Guide people in their decision-making as they reach for this future

Let's take them separately.

Vision Statement: *A description of the business as you want it to be.*

Your vision statement should talk about your business in its future state, communicating both the purpose and values of the organization and serving as a clear guide for choosing both the current and future courses of action. It doesn't say how you are going to get there, just where you are going, which sets the direction for your strategic planning.

Gone to the Dogs

Vision Statement
We will to be the second home for pets in Concordia, MA by providing them with individual attention and treating them as if they were our own, thereby ensuring peace of mind for pet owners when they have to leave their family members behind.

Mission Statement: *A statement describing a company's function, markets and competitive advantages.*

Your mission statement should reveal what the business is going to do, cover the customer groups being served, as well as the customer need being met (your products and services), describe the geographical location in which you are going to operate and indicate how you will measure success.

Remember, it is more important to communicate your mission statement to employees than to customers because your employees will personify the mission.

Gone to the Dogs

Mission Statement
We will become the second home for our customers pets, by understanding the needs of each pet and offering individual attention like a loving owner, and along with the highest quality pet food and products

for purchase.

Goals

A business may have a number of goals, each describing a desired future condition toward which efforts are directed. The starting point in writing business goals is to ask, "What do we need to do to accomplish our mission." In other words, a mission statement says "what" and business goals say "how."

For example, how will you understand the needs of each pet? One way would be to keep copious notes on each pet's individual likes, dislikes, habits and fears. So one of your goals could be to build a profile of each pet you care for. This section can also reflect the business's financial goals.

Gone to the Dogs

Business Goals

- Build and maintain a profile of each pet we care for.
- Stay current on health and fitness trends for dogs.
- Listen to and implement customer suggestions for improvement.

Financial Goals

- Achieve year one revenues of $499K with after tax profit of $136K.
- Achieve year two revenues of $565K with after tax profit of $172K.
- Achieve year three revenues of $641K with after tax profit of $213K.

Operational Design

Operational design is the outline of your business. To create this section, you need to answer a few basic questions. While the questions seem simple, answering them may not be. Don't get discouraged if it takes some time to answer them. You are creating the framework of your business.

If you have a clear idea of what the business will look like when it begins operations, this section should be fairly straight forward. If you are confused about how to proceed, we encourage you to work through the Visioning chapter of Part 1 to make your ideas more concrete. If you have completed part 1 of this book, you will use the information in your dream book to complete this section.

The output of this section is:

- The content for your Operations section
- A list of basic parameters for use in your financial model

The steps below are the ones we follow to quickly determine an operating model. We provide three examples, but obviously there are limitless variations. We will be using the three examples we discussed in the previous chapter to give you an idea of how to approach writing the section for your own business idea. At the end of this section, we will show you what a completed operation section of a business plan looks like.

1. State what the business does in a few, clearly worded sentences:

> Gone to the Dogs is a pet day care and grooming service focusing on the needs of frequent business travelers.
>
> Astro Hydraulics produces oleo struts for use in the fabrication of business jet landing gear. Its primary customers are Cessna, Piper and Hawker Aircraft owners.
>
> On Your Side is a business coaching service working with owners of small, merchant businesses to improve their companies.

Don't worry about going into detail about the products and services of your business as you will cover that in another section of your plan.

Give the location of the business and the type of facility it is housed in. If you don't have a fixed place of business, discuss your service area:

Gone to the Dogs, location not selected yet

It will be housed in roughly in 2,600 sq. ft. of commercial/retail space in a strip mall in the Harbor Isle area of Concordia, MA.

Astro Hydraulics, location known

Astro's facility will be a 12,000 sq. ft. shop floor located in an extension of the company's existing building at John Wayne Airport in Orange County, CA.

On Your Side, home based

Coaching services are provided at the client's place of business which can be anywhere within a fifty mile radius from the owner's home office in Del Rio, TX.

2. Detail the hours of operation:

Gone to the Dogs will be open:

Mon-Fri 6am – 6pm
Sat 8am – 6pm
Closed Sunday

Astro Hydraulics operates two shifts, 8 am to 4 pm and 4 pm to 12 am, Monday through Friday. Maintenance and retooling is usually performed during a six hour shift (10 am to 4 pm) on Saturdays. The plant can gear up to seven day operations if required.

131

On Your Side's scheduling is driven by client needs. Frequently appointments are scheduled in the evening or on weekends to accommodate the client's schedule and workload.

3. Discuss the number and type of employees or other assistance you think you'll need:

Gone to the Dogs

The company will employ workers who have a soft spot for pets. It is anticipated that four dog walkers and two inside staff will be hired to start the business.

Astro Hydraulics

The additional manufacturing capacity will require that the company hire about 20 new workers. Half of them will be skilled workers (machinists, CNC programmers) and the balance will be semi-skilled (assemblers, testers, and shipping clerks).

On Your Side

The company is a one person operation that will utilize the services of specialists as required by client needs.

4. List the company's products and services, specifically. While you won't need to detail this until you write the *'Products and Services'* section, you will need it for your financial modeling to determine the number and types of revenue streams.

Gone to the Dogs
Pet sitting - your home
Pet sitting – our kennel
Dog washing and grooming
High end pet food
Pet accessories and supplies

The sentence you will put in your plan:
Gone to the Dogs provides in-home and kennel pet sitting services, and grooming along with the finest pet food and supplies available.

Astro Hydraulics
Oleo struts and attachment hardware for:
Cessna Mustang
Piper Jet
Hawker 400, 600 and 800
Replacement Parts

Sentence in plan:
Astro provides quality oleo struts and hardware for a variety of aircraft including the Cessna Mustang, Piper Jet and Hawker 400, 600 and 800 series aircraft as well as providing maintenance spares and parts.

On Your Side
Accountability and Problem solving
Access to experts

Sentence in plan:
On Your Side assists small business owners by helping them set goals and holding them accountable for reaching them. We also help you solve your business problems by providing a separate, experienced point of view. For those problems needing expert help, we have access to experts in a variety of fields.

5. Discuss who you think your customer is. While this may change over the course of writing the business plan, start writing about who you believe you will be selling to at this point:

Gone to the Dogs

The company's main customers will be individuals with long

commutes or who have jobs that require extensive travel.

Astro Hydraulics

The company will sell its products directly to manufacturers and to jet maintenance companies through Casian Aerospace, an aftermarket aircraft parts distributor. The company has existing agreements with Casian.

On Your Side

Most of our customers will be sole proprietor businesses selling products and services to the public from retail locations.

6. While you won't use this next piece in the discussion of your operations, it's best to start thinking about it early. How many customers can you serve? *(If you don't know how to figure this out, keep going, as we will be discussing it in the next chapter).*

Gone to the Dogs

With the staffing currently contemplated, the company can service the equivalent of approximately 200 unique customers per year.

Astro Hydraulics

The new capability will allow Astro to increase its manufacturing capability depending on type of aircraft, from 7,000 to approximately 10,000 oleo struts per year. Each customer typically purchases three sets of struts per aircraft.

On Your Side

They will be able to handle about 50 individual clients per year.

Pulling the Operations Section Together

134

Take the individuals parts that you've written and assemble them into a single statement. Here is what our examples look like when completed:

Gone to the Dogs

Gone to the Dogs is a pet day care and grooming service focusing on the needs of frequent business travelers. It will be housed in roughly 2,600 sq. ft. of commercial/retail space in a strip mall in the Harbor Isle area of Concordia, MA.

Gone to the Dogs will be open:

Mon-Fri 6am – 6pm
Sat 8am – 6pm
Closed Sunday

Gone to the Dogs provides in-home and kennel pet sitting services, and grooming along with the finest pet food and supplies available. The company will employ workers who have a soft spot for pets. It is anticipated that four dog walkers and two inside staff will be hired to start the business.

The company's main customers will be individuals with long commutes or who have jobs that require extensive travel. With the staffing currently contemplated, the company can service approximately 200 customers per year.

Astro Hydraulics

Astro Hydraulics produces oleo struts for use in the fabrication of business jet landing gear. Its primary customers are Cessna, Piper and Hawker Aircraft owners. Astro's facility will be a 12,000 sq. ft. shop floor located in an extension of the company's existing building at John Wayne Airport in Orange County, CA.

Astro provides quality oleo struts and hardware for a variety of aircraft including the Cessna Mustang, Piper Jet and Hawker 400, 600 and 800 series aircraft as well as providing maintenance spares and parts. Astro Hydraulics operates on two shifts, 8 am to 4 pm and 4 pm to 12 am, Monday through Friday. Maintenance and retooling is usually performed during a six hour shift (10 am to 4 pm) on Saturdays. The plant can gear up to seven day operations if required.

The additional manufacturing capacity will require that the company hire about 20 new workers. Half of them will be skilled workers (machinists, CNC programmers) and the balance will be semi-skilled (assemblers, testers, shipping clerks).

The company will sell its products directly to manufacturers and to jet maintenance companies through Casian Aerospace, an aftermarket aircraft parts distributor. The company has existing agreements with Casian. The new capability will allow Astro to manufacture, depending on type of aircraft, from 7,000 to approximately 10,000, oleo struts per year. Each customer typically purchases three sets of struts per aircraft.

On Your Side

On Your Side is a business coaching service working with owners of small, merchant businesses. Coaching services are provided at the client's place of business which can be anywhere within a fifty mile radius from the owner's home office in Del Rio, TX.

On Your Side's scheduling is driven by client needs. Frequently appointments are scheduled in the evening or on weekends to accommodate the client's schedule and workload.

On Your Side assists small business owners by helping them set goals and holding them accountable for reaching them. We also help them solve their business problems by providing a separate, experienced point of view. For those problems needing expert help, we have access to experts in a variety of fields. The company is a one person operation that will utilize the services of specialists as required by client needs.

Most of their customers will be sole proprietor businesses selling products and services to the public from retail locations. We will be able to handle about 50 individual clients per year.

Products and Services

In this section you will describe in detail the products and services to be offered. Describe each service and product separately with their main characteristics and the benefits to the consumer. Here is what our examples look like when completed:

Gone to the Dogs

Pet sitting (your home) - While pet owners are away from their homes, a dog walker will take care of the pet at home. Two visits will be made during the day, in the morning, and at night. The walker will write up reports about the time spent with the pet for the owner's comfort. One copy will be for the pet's owner and another one for the company for quality control purposes.

Pet sitting (kennel) - Pet owners can leave their pets at the center while they are away. The pets will be taken out of the kennels several times during the day to play. The dogs will be segregated by temperament, weight and age, so low-activity dogs are not mixed with high-energy dogs. Each dog that comes into the center will be evaluated before being accepted to ensure the safety of all dogs. Dogs must be neutered and able to socialize with the other daycare residents and be up-to-date on their vaccinations.

Dog grooming - Grooming services will be available by appointment only. Grooming will include bathing, nail trimming, ear cleaning, hair cuts, trims and flea dipping. The pet owners can also request these services together with pet sitting. The grooming services will be performed by experienced groomers.

High quality pet food - The center will offer for sale quality food not offered in regular retail pet stores such as PetsMart and Target.

Pet accessories and supplies - Leashes, collars, clothing, hair accessories and other products will be available for sale.

Astro Hydraulics

Oleo struts and attachment hardware - Astro Hydraulics is known in its industry as the leader in aftermarket upgrade and replacement oleo struts for several small business jets including the Cessna Mustang, the Piper Jet and the Hawker 400, 600 and 800 series aircraft. Oleo struts are compressible pistons within the landing gear trucks of these aircraft that absorb the weight of the aircraft upon landing.

The chief difference in Astro's struts as opposed to the struts that are delivered as part of a new airframe is that Astro's proprietary, patented design allows for the strut to compress along its entire length in less than half the time of most original equipment struts. This, in turn, expands the performance envelope of the aircraft, allowing higher landing speeds and steeper approaches. An entire category of airports in close terrain will be serviceable by personal and small business jets.

Astro has been producing these struts since 1998 and several companies, such as Hawker, offer them as deliverable upgrades on new aircraft.

Repair and Maintenance Parts - Astro manufactures parts for both its own and manufacturer original equipment struts. In fact, the company is an Original Spares Manufacturer for every aircraft line it produces original struts for. The company will also perform depot maintenance for entire landing gear assemblies at it's plant at John Wayne Airport in Orange County, CA.

On Your Side

Accountability coaching - provides business owners with no-nonsense encouragement to help them stay focused on the activities required to achieve their goals. Weekly session combined with unlimited email support provide focus, direction and clarity.

Problem solving - using a combination of problem solving techniques and expert industry advice these sessions will be held in person and over the phone. The sessions will focus on finding creative solutions to the problems faced by business owners.

Fixed Plant and Assets

In this section you will describe the capital assets of the business. Plant, machinery and equipment, furniture and fixtures, and leasehold improvements comprise the fixed assets of most companies. This section is generally comprised of a short list.

Gone to the Dogs

The assets of Gone to the Dogs consist of furniture, computer equipment and fixtures. A detailed list can be found in the Financial Needs portion of the Executive Summary.

Chapter 17 - Financial Models

The Goal of This Chapter

To create a pro forma cash flow model for your business idea

What You Will Do in This Chapter

Gather the information needed to complete a pro forma cash flow projection using a template provided.

What You Will Have When You're Done

A completed three year pro forma cash flow projection
An understanding of the profit the business can make
A completed assumptions section for your business plan

Benefits of a cash flow model

A pro forma cash flow, also called a financial projection, is a document that predicts the financial performance of a business. It can be used as a forecast and for tracking results after your company is running. A properly done pro forma model will:

- Forecast revenue, expenses, cost of goods and net income
- Show trends and seasonality in revenue
- Identify cash infusions needed
- Uncover challenges to your goals
- Reveal how much capital you need to operate
- Predict income for the next three years

A cash flow model is important to the owner of the business because it gives a view into the financial future of a business. Taking time to estimate the costs of doing business allows you to realistically view the profitability of your business and avoid potential problems early.

What Do I Need To Know?

1. What your product or service will sell for
2. The cost to produce your product or service
3. The expenses your business will incur
4. Your start up costs. You will use these, plus an allowance for operating capital reserves, to determine the amount of investment or loan you will need to secure

Building Your Start Up Costs

One of the most important reasons to work through a visualization process is so you can figure your start up costs. In the visualization process you imagine what your business will look like and how it will operate. A byproduct of this effort should be a preliminary list of equipment, furnishings and tenant improvements needed to make your space ready for customers. If you have service business, visualizing the services will let you know the equipment needed to provide it to your customers. But if you have a space that you will decorate to make it appealing to your customers, then you will have some serious thinking to do. The amount of money you can spend to get a selling space to appear the way you want it to is nearly unlimited. Yet, the amount of money that you can get to create that space is limited by what you can borrow or convince investors to give you. It is also limited by the cash flow that will be created by the business for repayment.

For those with office or retail space one of the biggest items on your list in terms of cost will be your tenant improvements. Tenant improvements are changes to leased retail or commercial space to make them fit your vision for your company. It can take the form of adding or removing walls, creating built in shelving or storage or combining two existing spaces. It's hard to get an idea of what tenant improvements will cost until you are close to selecting a space, but you should set an *absolute* budget of what you will spend on improvements before you even go looking at property. That way you won't let your imagination run away with you when you encounter a space that could be *'perfect, if only'*.

It is important that you get your lists of things you need worked out early and begin pricing the items on them as soon as practical. Below is a list of the items needed by Gone to the Dogs, our doggie day care:

Tenant Improvements	
Demolition and construction of walls	$5,500
Air Conditioning Upgrades	3,500
Rubberized Floor 1,000 sq ft x $3.00	3,000
Kennels to house 100 dogs	13,500
Dog Washing/Grooming Stations (2)	5,000
Dog Washing Accessories (dryers, clippers)	3,500
Point of Sale (POS) System	3,500
Merchandise and Toys	10,000
Dog Food and Treats	8,000
Phone/Intercom System	4,500
Security Cameras and Web Cams	2,500
Office Furniture	5,500
Office Computer Equipment	2,500
Web Site Build	5,000
Working Capital (6 mos of expenses)	*100,634

Total Funds Needed	$176,134
Owner Injection	(26,134)
Funds Requested	$150,000

*Notice that you have a line item for six months expenses in your funds request. You will not be able to calculate that until you have built your pro forma cash flow. So when completing your start up expenses, leave that line open until you have an idea of what your monthly operating expenses will be. *Ask for at least four months, and preferably six months, of operating expenses coverage.*

Also notice there is a line labeled "owner injection" that reduces the amount of money from the funding source. This is a requirement of nearly all bank loans, especially SBA who by policy requires 30% of the money provided by you so you have a stake in the business. You may be able to negotiate a lesser percentage, but it will be substantial.

Selecting furnishings and equipment can be a make or break point for a start up business. Your surroundings need be to appropriate to your customer. Spending too much puts you in a hole to dig out of. Spend too little and you will not attract the customers you seek. It's a fine line to walk and you should revisit your decisions frequently as you develop information about your customers and target market.

Pro Forma Cash Flow Model

Gone to the Dogs Year 1 Pro Forma Cash Flow

	Factor 1	Factor 2	Jan	Feb	Mar	Apr	May	Jun	Jul	Aug	Sep	Oct	Nov	Dec	Total
Working Days ==>	25	25	25	25	25	25	25	25	25	25	25	25	25	25	300
Seasonality ==>	5%	5%	5%	5%	5%	5%	10%	12%	12%	10%	8%	8%	8%	12%	100%
	Avg Sale	Sales/Yr	Jan	Feb	Mar	Apr	May	Jun	Jul	Aug	Sep	Oct	Nov	Dec	Total
Revenue															
In Home Pet Services	20	5000	5,000	5,000	5,000	5,000	10,000	12,000	12,000	10,000	8,000	8,000	8,000	12,000	100,000
Doggie Day Care	16.32	15263	12,455	12,455	12,455	12,455	24,909	29,891	29,891	24,909	19,927	19,927	19,927	29,891	249,092
Grooming	55.5	1802	5,001	5,001	5,001	5,001	10,001	12,001	12,001	10,001	8,001	8,001	8,001	12,001	100,011
Merchandise	10	5000	2,500	2,500	2,500	2,500	5,000	6,000	6,000	5,000	4,000	4,000	4,000	6,000	50,000
Total Revenue			24,956	24,956	24,956	24,956	49,910	59,892	59,892	49,910	39,928	39,928	39,928	59,892	499,103
Cost of Goods Sold															
Grooming Wages	35	1802	3,154	3,154	3,154	3,154	6,307	7,568	7,568	6,307	5,046	5,046	5,046	7,568	63,070
Total Grooming Costs			3,154	3,154	3,154	3,154	6,307	7,568	7,568	6,307	5,046	5,046	5,046	7,568	63,070
Merchandise Purchases	5	5000	1,250	1,250	1,250	1,250	2,500	3,000	3,000	2,500	2,000	2,000	2,000	3,000	25,000
Total Merchandise Costs			1,250	1,250	1,250	1,250	2,500	3,000	3,000	2,500	2,000	2,000	2,000	3,000	25,000
Total Cost of Goods Sold			4,467	4,467	4,467	4,467	8,933	10,720	10,720	8,933	7,147	7,147	7,147	10,720	89,331
Gross Profit			20,489	20,489	20,489	20,489	40,977	49,173	49,173	40,977	32,782	32,782	32,782	49,173	409,772
			82%	82%	82%	82%	82%	82%	82%	82%	82%	82%	82%	82%	82%
Expenses															
Indirect Wages	95472	Annual	7,956	7,956	7,956	7,956	7,956	7,956	7,956	7,956	7,956	7,956	7,956	7,956	95,472
Indirect Payroll	17%	% Wages	1,353	1,353	1,353	1,353	1,353	1,353	1,353	1,353	1,353	1,353	1,353	1,353	16,230
Indirect Workers Compensation	3%	% Wages	239	239	239	239	239	239	239	239	239	239	239	239	2,864
Accounting	2500	Estimate	208	208	208	208	208	208	208	208	208	208	208	208	2,500
Advertising/Promotions	10000	Estimate	833	833	833	833	833	833	833	833	833	833	833	833	10,000
Bank Charges	500	Estimate	42	42	42	42	42	42	42	42	42	42	42	42	500
Consulting/Professional Services	2500	Estimate	208	208	208	208	208	208	208	208	208	208	208	208	2,500
Entertainment/Business Meals	2500	Estimate	208	208	208	208	208	208	208	208	208	208	208	208	2,500
Employee Recognition	1000	Estimate	83	83	83	83	83	83	83	83	83	83	83	83	1,000
Insurance - Liability	2000	Estimate	167	167	167	167	167	167	167	167	167	167	167	167	2,000
Lease/Rent	30000	Estimate	2,500	2,500	2,500	2,500	2,500	2,500	2,500	2,500	2,500	2,500	2,500	2,500	30,000
Licenses and Permits	1500	Estimate	125	125	125	125	125	125	125	125	125	125	125	125	1,500
Merchant Fees	0.03	% Revenue	749	749	749	749	1,497	1,797	1,797	1,497	1,198	1,198	1,198	1,797	14,973
Office Supplies/Expense	1200	Estimate	100	100	100	100	100	100	100	100	100	100	100	100	1,200
Printing and Reproduction	2500	Estimate	208	208	208	208	208	208	208	208	208	208	208	208	2,500
Postage	600	Estimate	50	50	50	50	50	50	50	50	50	50	50	50	600
Repairs and Maintenance	1500	Estimate	125	125	125	125	125	125	125	125	125	125	125	125	1,500
Security	120	Estimate	10	10	10	10	10	10	10	10	10	10	10	10	120
Telephone	4500	Estimate	375	375	375	375	375	375	375	375	375	375	375	375	4,500
Utilities	10000	Estimate	833	833	833	833	833	833	833	833	833	833	833	833	10,000
Website/E-Commerce	1200	Estimate	100	100	100	100	100	100	100	100	100	100	100	100	1,200
Total Expenses			16,473	16,473	16,473	16,473	17,221	17,521	17,521	17,221	16,922	16,922	16,922	17,521	203,659
Net Operating Income			4,016	4,016	4,016	4,016	23,756	31,652	31,652	23,756	15,860	15,860	15,860	31,652	206,112
			10%	16%	16%	16%	48%	53%	53%	48%	40%	40%	40%	53%	41%
	Rate	Amount													
Debt Service	6%	150000	2,227	2,227	2,227	2,227	2,227	2,227	2,227	2,227	2,227	2,227	2,227	2,227	26,724
EBIT			1,789	1,789	1,789	1,789	21,529	29,425	29,425	21,529	13,633	13,633	13,633	29,425	179,388
			7%	7%	7%	7%	43%	49%	49%	43%	34%	34%	34%	49%	36%
	State	Federal													
Income Tax	9%	15%			10,763			10,763			10,763			10,763	43,053
Net Income			1,789	1,789	-8,974	1,789	21,529	18,662	29,425	21,529	2,870	13,633	13,633	18,662	136,335
			7%	7%	-36%	7%	43%	31%	49%	43%	7%	34%	34%	31%	27%
Cumulative Cash Flow			1,789	3,578	5,396	-3,607	17,922	36,584	66,009	87,538	90,407	104,040	117,673	136,335	

Don't be afraid. We will take you step by step through creating your pro forma. You should open the model provided at *www.killerbusinessplan.com* so you can follow along with the discussion. See *"How to Use this Book"* for access details. If you go to the case study, you will see how each of the numbers were derived, exactly.

NOTE: The easiest way to complete this section will be to watch the videos that are supplied at the 'Electronic Materials' page of the *www.killerbusinessplan.com* website. Each video develops and expands the topics discussed here in greater detail.

Pro Forma Cash Flow Projection Breakdown

About Pro Forma Financials

1. All pro formas are guesses. The more you ground them in reality the better you will feel. *The information you develop are your assumptions.*

2. Consider carefully the assumptions you base your estimates on, and check them frequently. Keep them realistic.

3. Check the number of transactions you must make to achieve your forecast. Break it down to sales per hour if need be. If you are comfortable with the number of transactions needed, your model is probably okay.

4. The difference between you and a MBA star financial analyst is *you know you don't know what you are doing.* An MBA knows a lot of history and has an arsenal of formulas and assumptions that apply to that history, but their ability to see what is coming is *exactly equal to yours*. In fact, because they often defer to perceived authority, they actually have less vision than someone fresh to the field. For example, how many of your friends thought stated income loans were crazy at the same time real estate analysts were saying the boom was endless? I rest my case.

We have provided 10 different pro forma cash flow models for your use. The one you pick will be based on the number of revenue streams your business has.

You can see all these sections in action in the videos at *www.killerbusienessplan.com*. The examples follow Case Study 1- Gone to the Dogs. We tell you where you need to provide information. The information below is expanded in the videos. It truly is a case where a video is worth a million words.

Financial Assumptions

The financial assumptions are the first set of information included in the 'Financials' section of your business plan. This section of the plan is where you record all of the logic and formulas you used to create your financial projections. Detail them as far as possible. It shows that you've planned your business and researched its operations and you're prepared to run to that plan. The example below looks a lot like the exercise we went through in Case Study 1 - Gone to the Dogs. That's because all of the things you do to arrive at the numbers you put in your pro forma should be written down as you develop the plan so you can review whether they make sense over time.

   It is the same information we worked through in the case study videos condensed down:

Gone to the Dogs

Revenue

Year One revenue goal: $500,000

Revenue Streams

Visiting and walking dogs left at home by their owners while traveling
Caring for dogs at the company's location
Bathing and grooming dogs
Selling merchandise

Revenue Mix

At home dogs	20%	$100,000
On site dogs	50%	$250,000
Bathing/Grooming	20%	$100,000
Merchandise	10%	$50,000

Revenue Stream 1 - In Home Visits

In home visits are $20 per visit. To determine the number of visits required: $100,000 / $20 = 5,000 visits per year

Revenue Stream 2 - Doggie Day Care

Revenue mix estimate, based on the mix for each 100 dogs served:

Lap dog	$15 x 60 =	900.00	60%
Medium dog	$17.50 x 25 =	437.50	25%
Large dog	$20.00 x 15 =	300.00	15%
Total Revenue,	100 dogs	$1,637.50	100%

That means that the average charge per dog is $16.38.

To determine the number of average dogs required to meet revenue targets: $250,000 / $16.38 = 15,263 dogs per year.

To check this number, we make this check calculation: The facility will be open a total of 312 days per year. This means the business will need to serve an average of 49 dogs per day to meet its projections. The facility can handle up to 100 dogs per day.

Revenue Stream 3 - Grooming

Revenue mix estimate, based on the mix for each 100 dogs served:

Lap dog	$50 x 60 =	3,000.00	60%
Medium dog	$60 x 25 =	1,500.00	25%
Large dog	$70 x 15 =	1,050.00	15%
Total Revenue,	100 dogs	$5,550.00	100%

This gives us an average ticket of $55.50 per dog serviced. To determine the number of grooming appointments that must be made to make the revenue estimate:

$100,000 / $55.50 = 1,802 appointments per year.

Revenue Stream 4 - Merchandise

It is estimated that each sale will be an average of $10.00. To determine the total number of sales to meet the revenue estimate:

$5,000 / $10 = 50,000 total sales.

Cost of Goods Sold

Revenue Stream 1 - In Home Visits

Dog walker mileage only:

2 walkers x $5.00 x 9 trips x 5 days x 52 weeks = $23,400 in mileage per year (purchases).

Revenue Stream 3 - Grooming

GTTD will pay contract groomers $35.00/hours for each dog served. 2 groomers x $35.00/dog x 1802 dogs/year = $63,070 direct purchases per year.

Revenue Stream 4 - Merchandise

GTTD will market up its merchandise 100% (double the price) for each item sold. Therefore, each item costs $5.00

$5.00/sale x 5,000 sales = $25,000 in direct purchases per year.

Expenses

Indirect wages consists of both direct and indirect functions as these personnel are assigned both revenue and overhead duties:

2 walkers x $8.50/hr x 40 hrs/week x 52 weeks = $35,360 total walker wages 2 in house employees x $8.50/hr x 68 hrs/week x 52 weeks = $60,112 total in house staff wages.

Amount entered in indirect wages = $95,472.

Indirect payroll expense

17% is selected to cover employer's portion of taxes, social security and disability burden.

Workers Compensation

3% is selected based on a cost estimate from a commercial insurer

The balance of expense items are best estimates based on research. Rent is based on actual location under negotiation in Concordia, MA.

Debt Service is estimated based on Use of Funds amount of $150,000 at 6% interest for a term of seven years.

Income Tax is estimated based on prevailing rates per interview with our CPA.

REVENUE (You must provide data)

Revenue is all monies received from the sales of products and/or services.

	Factor 1	Factor 2	Jan	Feb	Ma		Dec	Total
Revenue	Avg Sale	Sales/Yr						
In Home Pet Services	20	5000	5,000	5,000			12,000	100,000
Doggie Day Care	16.32	15263	12,455	12,455	...		29,891	249,092
Grooming	55.5	1802	5,001	5,001		8,001	12,001	100,011
Merchandise	10	5000	2,500	2,500		4,000	6,000	50,000
Total Revenue			24,955	24,955		9,928	59,892	499,103

Most businesses make money from selling more than one thing. In fact, most retail businesses make revenue by selling many things. Looking at all of the things you're selling may make creating a forecast seem daunting but it can be simplified to the point where it's manageable. **The important thing is that you do it.**

The different ways that businesses create revenue are called *revenue streams*. A revenue stream is an item or a group of items that are sufficiently alike that you can gather their earnings into a single category. Generally, you can gather items together if they have similar prices and similar costs. Collecting similar items into a single revenue stream makes forecasting your revenue easier.

In order to make this concept easier to grasp, we will be continuing the case studies from the previous section to demonstrate how to decide if you need multiple revenue streams. The examples give you a very detailed discussion regarding how numbers are derived. Even if the business in the examples are far from your idea, the concepts are the same.

Each stream of revenue includes all income made from each product or service offering. The average price of the product or service must be determined, followed by a projected number of sales per year. Once the two factors are multiplied for each stream, the final sum is the year's total revenue. It is then divided back out over the months using 'seasonality'.

SEASONALITY (You must calculate)

Seasonality ==>		5%	5%	. . .	8%	12%	100%
Factor 1	Factor 2	Jan	Feb	Mr	Dec	Total

Across the top of the spreadsheet is a row of percentages. The numbers represent the percentage of annual income expected each month for revenue and cost of goods purposes. If your product sells better in some months than in others, adjust the percentages to match how you will sell.

The number in the 'Total' column should be 100%. If it is not, adjust your percentages until it is.

Direct vs. Indirect Expenses

Before you think I'm being a wonk for bringing this up, understanding how to categorize costs is a major skill in staying in business.

There are two basic types of cost involved in any business.

Direct costs are those expenses that contribute directly to the product or service you sell. If you make televisions, then the parts, like the chassis and plastic shell, the electronic components and the wages of the people who assemble them are direct costs. If you didn't make the item, you wouldn't incur the cost. These are also called *variable costs*.

Indirect costs can be administrative or sales expense. Your sales force, your accounting team and management, they are indirect costs as are your rent, utilities, telephone expenses and the like. You will pay these expenses even if you don't sell a single thing. These are also called *fixed costs*.

Direct (variable) costs are recorded in the Costs of Goods Sold (COGS) section of the model because they are directly attributable to each dollar of sales. They are sometimes called **unavoidable costs** because you must incur them to have product to sell.

Indirect (fixed) costs are recorded in the expenses section of the model because they support the creation of your product and its sales. These types of expenses are collectively referred to as **overhead**. These are also known as avoidable costs because you can choose how to structure the support aspects of your company. For example, you can choose to have one person handle accounts payable, accounts receivable and payroll, or have a separate person for each.

If you have people in your plan that will do nothing but produce your product, or if you purchase items for resale, then you should record their wages or purchase prices in the COGS section of the model. Why? Because it shows the reader of your plan that you understand the difference between direct and indirect cost and are accounting for that difference. This will score points with bankers and underwriters.

If you have people that produce your product, but also do other administrative tasks, then record their wages in the expenses section of the model, unless you can clearly split the time they will spend in each place. If splitting the costs between the two categories makes the model too difficult to understand, then don't do it. Always choose clarity over being specific if simplifying your writing makes your message clearer.

Later on, when your business is in operation, having the costs broken up in to these categories will be invaluable when streamlining your operations and making them more profitable

COST OF GOODS SOLD-COGS (You must provide data)

	Factor 1	Factor 2	Jan	Feb	Ma		Dec	Total
Cost of Goods Sold								
Grooming Wages	35	1802	3,154	3,154		146	7,568	63,070
Total Grooming Costs			3,154	3,154	. . .	146	7,568	63,070
Merchandise Purchases	5	5000	1,250	1,250		100	3,000	25,000
Total Merchandise Costs			1,250	1,250		100	3,000	25,000
Total Cost of Goods Sold			4,467	4,467		47	10,720	89,331

Next, the cost of goods sold is determined. Each revenue stream is broken into two parts: Purchases and Wages.

Purchases represent the cost for any portion of what you make that is purchased whether it is a part or a subcontract service.

Wages include any amount of money paid to an employee to produce the product. These wages are directly linked to the product or service offering for each respective stream.

Note that the total sales are placed in the column marked, "Factor 2". All you do is apply the dollar amount of gross revenue that purchases and wages represent.

DIRECT PAYROLL TAXES AND WORKERS COMPENSATION (You must provide data)

See indirect payroll and workers' compensation, below for details as they are calculated the same way.

GROSS PROFIT (Calculated for you)

Revenue – COGS = Gross Profit.

	Factor 1	Factor 2	Jan	Feb	Ma		Dec	Total
Total Revenue			24,955	24,955		28	59,892	499,103
Minus								
Total Cost of Goods Sold			4,467	4,467	. . .	47	10,720	89,331
Equals								
Gross Profit			20,489	20,489		82	49,173	409,772
			82%	82%		2%	82%	82%

The 82% under the January column is the "Gross Margin" for that month. When you hear that term this is what it means.

EXPENSES (You must calculate)

Expenses, sometimes called indirect costs, are the items you will pay regardless of whether you have revenue or not.

Expenses include any expenditure made outside the direct cost of the specific product or service. These include indirect wages; all payment for labor not directly producing the product or service offering. Most businesses include some type of insurance expense, lease/rent, utilities, telephone, and advertising. For example, your receptionist or payroll clerk don't make your products and as such, are indirect employees.

Indirect Payroll Expense

	Factor 1	Factor 2	Jan	Fe		Dec	Total
Indirect Wages	95472	Annual	7,956	· · · 56		7,956	95,472
Indirect Payroll	17%	% Wages	1,353		53	1,353	16,230

You will need to research what payroll taxes are in your state. Total up the percentages and enter the amount in the Payroll box. Expenses for health insurance and other fringe benefits will be added to the expense section using other line items.

You can also apply a percentage amount that will cover all payroll taxes, insurance, vacation and other fringe benefits. Many businesses apply an industry standard, such as 30 to 40% of payroll. When you use this approach, you will not add any additional amounts for fringe benefits in the line items below, such as health insurance.

1. **Workers Compensation**

	Factor 1	Factor 2	Jan	Fe		Dec	Total
Indirect Workers Compensation	3%	% Wages	239	· · ·	39	239	2,864

If you have employees, you will likely have to pay worker's compensation. Worker's compensation is insurance to assist workers who are injured on the job. The amount you pay for this insurance is based on claims experience not only for your company, but for the industry as a whole. It is almost always charged as a percentage of payroll.

For example, the annual payment for workers compensation for a company whose employees are in an office setting would be much lower than for a company whose employees work on a construction site.

You can Google the topic to get a preliminary number to place in the box, but you should speak with an insurance broker to get pricing, enter the percentage in the 'Worker's Compensation' box.

2. Other Expenses

	Factor 1	Factor 2	Jan	Feb	Ma		Dec	Total
Expenses								
Accounting	2500	Estimate	208	208		08	208	2,500
Advertising/Promotions	10000	Estimate	833	833		33	833	10,000
Bank Charges	500	Estimate	42	42		42	42	500
Consulting/Professional Services	2500	Estimate	208	208		08	208	2,500
Entertainment/Business Meals	2500	Estimate	208	208		08	208	2,500
Employee Recognition	1000	Estimate	83	83		33	83	1,000
Insurance - Liability	2000	Estimate	167	167		57	167	2,000
Lease/Rent	30000	Estimate	2,500	2,500		00	2,500	30,000
Licenses and Permits	1500	Estimate	125	125	▪ ▪ ▪	25	125	1,500
Merchant Fees	0.03	% Revenue	749	749		98	1,797	14,973
Office Supplies/Expense	1200	Estimate	100	100		00	100	1,200
Printing and Reproduction	2500	Estimate	208	208		08	208	2,500
Postage	600	Estimate	50	50		50	50	600
Repairs and Maintenance	1500	Estimate	125	125		25	125	1,500
Security	120	Estimate	10	10		10	10	120
Telephone	4500	Estimate	375	375		75	375	4,500
Utilities	10000	Estimate	833	833		33	833	10,000
Website/E-Commerce	1200	Estimate	100	100		00	100	1,200
Total Expenses			16,473	16,473		?2	17,521	203,659

The expenses shown in the chart above are representative of many businesses but may not represent all the expenses you will have. In those cases, you may have to add lines by copying them or reuse lines you don't need.

Any line items you don't use, simply zero out and hide the line.

NET OPERATING INCOME (Calculated for you)

Gross Profit – Expenses = Net Operating Income

	Factor 1	Factor 2	Jan	Feb	Ma		Dec	Total
Gross Profit			20,489	20,489		82	49,173	409,772
Minus								
Total Expenses			16,473	16,473	· · ·	22	17,521	203,659
Equals								
Net Operating Income			4,016	4,016		60	31,652	206,112
			16%	16%		)%	53%	41%

DEBT SERVICE (You must provide data)

	Factor 1	Factor 2	Jan	Feb	Ma		Dec	Total
	Rate	Amount				· · ·		
Debt Service	6%	150000	2,227	2,227		27	2,227	26,724

The Debt Service is the amount of your payment for a business loan. The rate is the percentage of interest that is paid back annually. THESE ARE NOT AUTO CALCUATED FIELDS. To find the monthly payment, go to a website such as Bankrate.com and use one of the available mortgage calculators, and plug the resulting payment into each month.

EBIT – EARNINGS BEFORE INTEREST & TAX (Calculated for you)

Net Operating Income – Debit Service = EBIT

	Factor 1	Factor 2	Jan	Feb	Ma		Dec	Total
Net Operating Income			4,016	4,016		60	31,652	206,112
Minus								
Debt Service	6%	150000	2,227	2,227	· · ·27		2,227	26,724
Equals								
EBIT			1,789	1,789		33	29,425	179,388
			7%	7%		i%	49%	36%

INCOME TAX (You must provide data)

	Factor 1	Factor 2	Jan	Feb	Ma		Dec	Total
	State	Federal			▪ ▪ ▪			
Income Tax	9%	15%					10,763	43,053

Income Tax is the primary source of revenue for the federal government and many states. Both corporations and individuals are subject to income taxes on their net profit. Enter the rate that you think you will be taxed at. Contact your state taxing authority or the IRS for specific percentages.

NET INCOME (Calculated for you)

EBIT - INCOME TAX = NET INCOME

	Factor 1	Factor 2	Jan	Feb	Ma		Dec	Total
EBIT			1,789	1,789	;33		29,425	179,388
Minus								
Income Tax	9%	15%			▪ ▪ ▪		10,763	43,053
Equals								
Net Income			1,789	1,789	;33		18,662	136,335
			7%	7%	4%		31%	27%

This is the amount, post tax that your company will earn. You should have no further deductions from this amount. Please note that the projection does not deduct depreciation or other non cash items.

Depreciation and amortization are concepts that effect the tax you pay and represent the declining usefulness of your business assets. They are important concepts to master as a business owner but they do not affect cash flow and are of minor importance to a start up business. You will need to understand these concepts once you are launched and a good CPA will be able to explain them to you. We have never had a business plan questioned because we didn't forecast these items.

CUMULATIVE CASH FLOW (Calculated for you)

	Factor 1	Factor 2	Jan	Feb	M		Dec	Total
Net Income			1,789	1,789	...		18,662	136,335
The results from each month are added up to reveal cumulative earnings								
Cumulative Cash Flow			1,789	3,578				136,335

Cumulative cash flow shows the amount of net income as it builds month to month:

Chapter 18 - Industry Research

The Goal of This Chapter

Determine the industry your business is in, including its North America
Industry Classification System code (NAICS)
Discover the trends in your industry

What You Will Do in This Chapter

Use the U.S. Census Bureau to find your NAICS code
Research the latest trends for your industry

What You Will Have When You're Done

Your NAICS code and description
Description of the industry your business is in
Current and future trends in your industry

Industry

An industry is defined as a group of companies offering products or
services that are similar and that satisfy the same basic customer needs.
The first step to researching a specific industry is learning the size and
nature of the industry. This is accomplished by researching statistics
and the companies in your industry. The best way to find this
information is using government, trade and industry resources.

All businesses registered in Canada, Mexico and the United States
fall under a NAICS code (North American Industry Classification
System). NAICS is a business industry code used by the government to
classify and measure economic activity. This system replaced the
Standard Industry Code (SIC) system. *This code is also used by banks
when processing a loan request.* The banks compare your projected
cash flow, with similar businesses by using your NAICS code. If you

do not supply a NAICS code, the underwriter will choose one, which may or may not work to your advantage. That's why it is very important that you get your NAICS code right.

All NAICS classifications on U.S. businesses may be found on the U.S. Census website. You can search by business activity or NAICS code. The government is a great source of industry information, but as a caution, be sure to check the age of the data. 10 year old information will not benefit you. Certainly any information from the 2004-2007 economic boom would be valueless at this point. You should look for data that was gathered no more than 2-3 years ago if possible.

Simply searching the web using keywords such as "restaurant industry statistics", or using search engines to search by NAICS code can produce helpful information. Many times you can find scholarly articles and valid sources concerning your target industry through library databases as well.

Below are samples of the NAICS codes selected for each company. The definitions used are directly from the U.S. Census Bureau website *(www.census.gov/naics/)*.

Gone to the Dogs

NAICS code was researched using the keyword 'grooming.' There is only one code for this type of service and it is a good match for Gone to the Dogs services

812910 Pet Care (except Veterinary) Services
This industry comprises establishments primarily engaged in providing pet care services (except veterinary), such as boarding, grooming, sitting, and training pets.

Astro Hydraulics

This NAICS code was researched using the keywords 'aircraft parts'. There are three NAICS codes with the keywords 'aircraft' and 'parts'; for wholesalers, aircraft parts and engine parts. The aircraft parts is the closest description to Astro Hydraulics.

336413 Other Aircraft Parts and Auxiliary Equipment

Manufacturing
This U.S. industry comprises establishment primarily engaged in (1) manufacturing aircraft parts or auxiliary equipment (except engines and aircraft fluid power subassemblies) and/or (2) developing and making prototypes of aircraft parts and auxiliary equipment. Auxiliary equipment includes such items as crop dusting apparatus, armament racks, in-flight refueling equipment, and external fuel tanks.

On Your Side

There is no NAICS code for business coaching. The best match for On Your Side was with the keywords 'business consulting'.

541611 Administrative Management and General Management Consulting Services
This U.S. industry comprises establishments primarily engaged in providing operating advice and assistance to businesses and other organizations on administrative management issues, such as financial planning and budgeting, equity and asset management, records management, office planning, strategic and organizational planning, site selection, new business startup, and business process improvement. This industry also includes establishments of general management consultants that provide a full range of administrative; human resource; marketing; process, physical distribution, and logistics; or other management consulting services to clients.

If you are taking your plan for funding, statistics on the industry at a national, state, county and city level give the underwriter grounding. Since the underwriter reviewing your business plan is key to approving your loan request you want to give them as much favorable information as possible. If the underwriter has to do their own research they may find information that is not in your favor.

Also note that you need to be grounded as well. Underwriters are people, and frequently they have their own biases. For example, we had one case when an underwriter had a specific dislike of a certain consumer product, so she denied the loan request. You must be able to defend your business idea with good market analysis.

Industry Trends

Industry trends indicate the performance of an industry and the direction it is moving. While doing your industry research, pay careful attention to any trends whether negative or positive. It is important to be aware of the trends that affect your business. What is selling the most? Is the industry declining? What are the customers demanding? What is starting to become popular? After analyzing industry trends, you may be able to identify a niche for your business. You may also decide to modify your products/services to meet the current industry trends.

SWOT Analysis

SWOT analysis is a strategic planning tool that is utilized by organizations to ensure that all factors related to a project or business are identified and addressed. SWOT stands for: strengths, weaknesses, opportunities and threats. Factors affecting the success of the project are both internal and external.

Strengths - look for the things that will enable the ultimate success of the project. An experienced management team would be considered a strength.

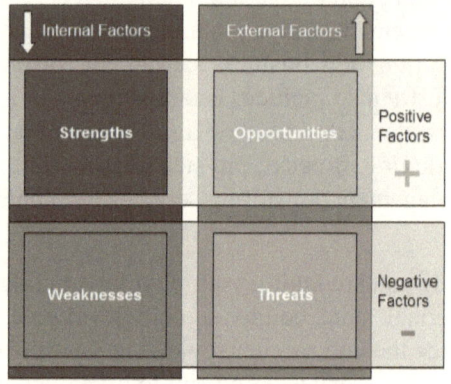

Weaknesses - look for things that could prevent success. A lack of adequate funding would be considered a weakness that could ultimately shut down the business.

Opportunities - these are the ways, and market, where you will sell your product or advance your project. Market conditions could be prime for your new venture, or you could already have several committed customers who will purchase your product.

Threats - look for factors that could inhibit or stop your project. Maybe you are thinking of opening a bank, but there is a negative public perception of banks. In addition, the regulatory environment is vague

160

and likely to become more difficult. This would be a threat to your new venture.

Use these definitions to gather a list of the factors affecting your business. Once you have that list, you will want to review them by applying the USED acronym of a SWOT Analysis.

Consider how to **USE** each strength, **STOP** each weakness, **EXPLOIT** each opportunity and **DEFEND** against each threat.

You will find you are unable to control all of the forces that will affect your business. You should then decide if your business can adapt overtime to those uncontrollable forces, or if you need to make changes to your business model or business idea.

As you work through your business plan, keep your SWOT analysis handy, so you continue to identify and add issues (both positive and negative) that arise as you plan your business launch.

Industry Description

After you have completed your industry research, including determining the correct NAICS code and market trends, you can begin a draft of the 'Industry Description' for your business plan. Below is a sample of the 'Industry Description' section for Gone to the Dogs.

812910 Pet Care (except Veterinary) Services
This industry comprises establishments primarily engaged in providing pet care services (except veterinary), such as boarding, grooming, sitting, and training pets.

In 2010, the pet industry in the U.S. is estimated to reach $47.7 billion according to the American Pet Products Association (APPA). Pet grooming and boarding, will share $3.45 billion. Demand for pet services is a growing industry segment. Many pet owners are increasingly treating their pets as a family member. According to the 2009/2010 National Pet Owners Survey conducted by APPA, 62% of U.S. households, 71.4 million homes, own a pet. There are approximately 77.5 million dogs owned by 45.6 million homes and 93.6 million cats owned by 38.2 million households. According to the U.S. Census Bureau in 2007 there were 11,184 businesses engaged in the pet

care industry and 306 businesses in Massachusetts, with sales of $2.3 billion and $68.6 million, respectively.

Pet ownership has increased in recent years, especially for dogs. Empty nesters are adopting pets for companionship, and couples without children are substituting pets for them. Society is being continuously influenced by movies and Hollywood stars, and pet ownership hasn't been the exception. In several movies pets are the protagonists. For example, when Beverly Hills Chihuahua was popular there was an increased demand for that specific breed of dog. When Disney released the movie 101 Dalmatians, the demand for Dalmatian puppies went through the roof.

The demand for pet services and products has shifted from basic to luxury. The article "Pet Gifts Aren't Going Begging" , in the magazine Souvenirs, Gifts & Novelties, quotes from a pet center owner "treating pets like a member of the family, and buying them presents to show it, has become the rule rather than the exception over the past few years". A kennel is no longer acceptable by many pet owners leaving their pets behind while on vacation. They insist their pet be pampered at a pet hotel. The expenditure on pets has increased from $17 billion in 1997 to $47.7 billion in 2010. This growth is mainly attributed to the increased demand for high end products and services, with dogs showing the majority of growth. These products and services include designer clothing, jewelry, spas, hotels, day care and therapeutic massages. There are even regimes of physical therapy and medical treatment that rival human care in terms of quality and cost.

Pet service demand remains relatively strong despite the economic downturn. The overall trend during this period is value for price, which doesn't necessarily mean spending less.

Current Trends

Pets welcome
Many hotels now advertise themselves as "pet friendly." Several chains have added pet services and accommodations in their hotels including pet pillows, plush robes and treats. Some even have a licensed pet masseuse on staff.

Green products

There is a demand for green products from natural litters to toys, accessories and organic food options.

Designers
Brands traditionally known for human products are now offering pet products. Big name companies include Paul Mitchell, Harley Davidson and Old Navy. They offer products such as shampoo, pet attire and toys.

Retailers
Shopping for pet products is becoming easier as retailers expand their pet section. Companies such as Target and Wal Mart have expanded their selection in order to meet pet owner's demands.

Grooming sessions
A haircut and nail trim is not enough. Mouthwash and electric tooth brushing for dogs are becoming normal.

Stress relief
Dogs and cats are taken to toy gyms and spas to relieve stress.

On the Road
For automobile travel dog owners are purchasing harnesses, seat belt systems or portable carriers to keep their pets safe. Other products include waste disposal systems and motion sickness aids.

Chapter 19 - Customer Identification

The Goal of This Chapter

Identify your customer in detail

What You Will Do in This Chapter

Develop demographics and psychographics for your customer

What You Will Have When You're Done

A clear understanding of your customer plus the demographic information for your plan.

Who is Your Customer?

Customers are people that buy your product or service. Your customers will share common needs or characteristics that your company can serve. Once you define your customer, you aim your marketing activities towards them. No business can be all things to all people. Instead, you must target the specific customers who are likely to buy your product or service and satisfy their particular wants or needs.

This is the single most important question that you will ask yourself in the entire business plan process. It will determine what you stock, how you advertise and who you hire. It will set your hours of business, and what your location looks like. Every decision you will make about your business will be determined by the answer to this question. If, when asked the question, 'Who is your customer', your answer is 'everybody' or 'anybody with a pulse' or 'pulse optional if I can get a credit card number', then your chances of success are greatly diminished.

If you sell to *everyone* or *anyone*, you're selling to **no one**.

Corporations spend vast sums of time and treasure learning exactly who buys their products and tailor their marketing efforts precisely. And it's not just consumer product firms like Nike, Coke or Red Bull; esoteric consulting firms like MacKenzie and Booz Allen routinely perform market research to better understand and position their companies in the marketplace.

The process of finding and studying your customer does not have to be complex or expensive, but it is extremely important. It requires you to find out everything you can about the customers whom you intend to pursue. Once you have that information, you'll have a much better chance of attracting them.

The facts you need to know about your customer fall into these three categories:
- Customer Needs
- Demographics
- Geographics and Psychographics

Customer Needs

You need to ask yourself: What does my customer want? When they buy my product or service, what are the benefits they want to get out of it? What problem does it solve for them or help them avoid? The key to this is not to think of your customers as buying a product, but instead to think of them as buying the benefits they get from the product or service. This knowledge first comes from any experience you have in the business. Brainstorm with your partners or colleagues. Next, start asking your prospective customers what they want, through interviews or surveys.

Further information can be found in books, magazines and newspaper articles about the market and industry. The articles that you already have from part one of the book about your target market will have some important insights as to the wants and needs of your customers.

Demographics

The demographics of a population are its characteristics in terms of age, gender, income level, occupation, education, and family circumstances (married, single, retired, etc.). Understanding the demographics of your customer is important because their demographic characteristics are strongly related to their buying behavior. For example, if you are selling toys, are there enough families with young children near your store to buy your product? The answers to these important questions can be found, in part, by demographics.

There are several resources for researching the demographics of your customer. The internet is probably the most important tool that you will use in your research. The biggest issues with research on the internet are currency, relevance and accuracy. Most current business research is done for a fee and the information that is readily available is dated. As a general rule, it's tough to get by with research that is more than two years old or occurred before a major shift in the economy. For example, information about the economy or business in January 2008, although relatively timely, would not be useful in 2010 because the economy when through a drastic change in the fall of that year.

Since the most current information is going to be for pay, the best places to find that information are at sites that already paid for it. Frequently news sites will pay for business information and intelligence on which to base their articles. Searching sites such as The Wall Street Journal, Forbes, The Economist, Bloomberg and others will get you to some of the statistics that you're looking for. Further, the articles in these outlets will frequently give you the name of the source of data. You can then take that name and search for the source and find other mentions of the information you're seeking.

Finding accurate data can also be a problem. Using trusted sources goes a long way toward getting accurate data. If you are concerned about the accuracy of the data, you can cross check it using an internet search engine. The more hits you get with accompanying data that matches, the better you should feel about using the information.

Here are some search engines you can use for finding information about a specific topic on the internet. You put in a search topic, and they find and give you many results of websites and articles that are related to your topic. Each search engine is different, but only slightly and all are user friendly.

- Google- www.google.com

- Ask- www.ask.com
- Yahoo- www.yahoo.com
- Alexa- www.alexa.com
- Exalead- www.exalead.com/search
- Gigablast- www.gigablast.com
- Live Search- www.live.com

The key to using these search engines is using the right search terms. Use an advanced search to narrow down your results, using specific, not general terms. Sometimes asking a question is the best way to get information from a search engine. Remember to tell the search engine to exclude items you do not want in your results.

More resources for your research include:

- The website of the city that you are researching. For example, if you are researching the City of Ontario, go to their official website

- The U.S. Census Bureau. You can use their American Factfinder search engine, found on their website www.census.gov. This provides you with important demographic information about any city, county, state or region in the U.S.

The most important takeaway is to be creative. The information is out there, but it isn't generally easy to find and will take some time to get; plan on spending about four to eight hours researching your business on the internet.

Libraries

If you live near a large city or university, the libraries of these institutions can be a great resource. For example, many large city libraries can give you access to LexisNexis or a similar high end search tool simply by having a library card. Services like Lexus Nexus will have access to the results of many surveys and studies that won't be easily found on the internet. Sometimes you will find the results of paid studies in a search. Many big city and university libraries that don't offer access to paid search engines will perform the search for you on request. Check out the libraries near you to find out what services are available to their members.

Trade Organizations

Once you have established the industry you are in, you can research the trade organizations that support it. Many of these organizations are the buyers of paid research so they can offer the results to their members. You may need to join the organization to get access to the information, but in many cases it will be worth it.

Pulling the Customer Attributes Section Together

Below is the section that you would place in your *Customer Attributes* part of the business plan. What appears below is a minimum representation of what should be included in your plan. It's almost impossible to have too much information in this section. The more you have, the more comfortable you, and your funding source, will be.

Gone to the Dogs

Over 17 million U.S. households are considered premium pet owners; this is about one-third of all pet -owning households (71.4 million households own pets). They are the pet owners that most pamper their pets and consider them a member of the family.

The demographics for premium pet owners is divided into six distinct groups:

- Affluents (household income of $150K or more)
- Specialty shoppers (those purchasing pet supplies through pet stores or Internet only)
- Married with children (household income of $100K or more)
- Empty nesters (household income of $75K or more)
- Dual-income/no kids (household income of $75K or more)
- Singles (household income of $50K or more)

The clients for pet services providers, for the most part, are locals living within close proximity to them. Yet, there are pet owners willing to drive extra miles to ensure their pets receive the top of the line services and facilities. For most premium pet owners price is not an issue when selecting a kennel, as long as they can have peace of mind when leaving their pets under the kennel's care.

Geographics and Psychographics

Geographics looks at the characteristics of a population in a certain region or country of the world, market or climate. Psychographics are the characteristics of a population in terms of personality, motives, lifestyles and geodemographics (neighborhood lifestyles). Think of geographics as where your customers are and psychographics as how they live.

The purpose of looking at the geographics and psychographics is to be able to look at your customers and know where and how they live. This information helps you understand what they want and how to reach them.

Here are some resources for researching geographies and psychographics of a population:
- Search engines like Google and Yahoo.
- Books written about your target market.
- Magazine and newspaper articles; some sources include TIME, Newsweek, The New York Times, Los Angeles Times, Business Week.

Gone to the Dogs

According to the U.S. Census Bureau, the city of Concordia, Ma has a total of 573,463 households with a mean income of $76,545. Gone to the Dogs primary target will be households with $100K annual income or more. In Concordia, 24% of the households have incomes of $100K or above (137,631 households) and 16,000 households are families with incomes of $150K or more. These households match the demographics for the premium pet owners identified above: affluents, and married with children.

Chapter 20 - Marketing

The Goal of This Chapter

To provide an understanding of basic marketing techniques
Identify your competitors

What You Will Do in This Chapter

Learn about basic marketing techniques so you can create a marketing plan
Differentiate yourself from your competition

What You Will Have When You're Done

A basic marketing plan
Names and locations of your competition and how you will stand out relative to them.

What is the Difference Between Marketing and Sales?

Marketing is the process of identifying a target consumer for your product or service and creating the message, strategy and tactics to reach them.

Marketing is a creative activity. It encompasses advertising, public relations, brand and viral marketing. It is also concerned with anticipating the customers' future needs and wants, often determining them through market research. Marketing is fundamental to any businesses growth. Marketers have the task of creating consumer awareness of the products/services. Marketing is usually focused on one product or service and product development is usually considered part of marketing. Thus, a marketing plan for one product might be very different than that for another.

Sales are the activities involved in directly completing a transaction for products or services in return for money or other compensation. Sales engage the prospect directly to close the sale.

Sales is considered by many people to be a part of marketing, however, the two disciplines are completely different. The skills required to generate interest and those required to 'close' a sale are not the same. A creative marketer may not have a strong enough ego to be a good salesman. As a small business owner you must be able to do both.

Sales involve the following activities:
- Cultivating prospective buyers (or leads) in a market segment (cold calling and networking)
- Conveying the features, advantages and benefits of a product or service to the prospective buyers
- Closing the sale and coming to agreement on pricing and services

Why Perform Market Research

Market research is the systematic, objective, collection and analysis of data about a particular target market, competition, and/or environment. By gaining an understanding of these, you can better understand how to market to your customers, how your industry works, and how to position your business in the face of competition. This understanding enables you to compete effectively, attract customers, and keep them coming back. For these reasons market research is a fundamental tool for running an efficient, effective and profitable business.

Competition

Competitors of a business are other companies, usually in the same industry, that are striving to secure the business of customers by offering them products and services with similar terms or features. For new products or ideas, the biggest competitor can be the status quo, or what people are already doing. Changing human behavior is one of the hardest jobs there is, so your marketing message must be compelling.

Competitors are most likely targeting the same customers you are. It is important for you to understand who they are and their strategies and tactics so that you can respond to their competitive actions effectively, learn from them and apply them to your own business. To learn about your competitors, you must first identify who they are. Begin by making a list of your known competitors, then conduct further research to discover any competitors that you could be unaware of.

There are several resources you can use for finding and researching competitors:

- Search engines like Google and Yahoo
- Yellow pages, both the book and online
- Your competitors' websites
- Business lists from the city where your business resides
- SEC.gov. This website for the Securities and Exchange Commission has a variety of financial and other information for all publicly traded companies.
- Newspaper articles about the industry or your competitors
- Magazine articles about the industry or your competitors.
  - Look in magazines like TIME, Newsweek, Inc. and Fast Company as well as industry-specific magazines (Skater magazines if you sell skateboards, for example)

Even after starting your business, you need to stay plugged in and aware of your competition.

Differentiation

A lot of investors ask the question, 'What problem does your product solve?' This is a fair question for a brand new product or service. You should be able to quantify the customers' pain by speaking to the number of people affected by it or how much money or productivity is lost because of it. This is an especially relevant question for a new product or service because it has to overcome the *status quo* that is, will people do something different than what they've always done? If you don't have a compelling answer to that question, you may not be able to get investors, but that doesn't mean you don't have a business idea. Banks fund ideas that have a reasonable chance at success. But if you don't have a new problem to solve, you do have to have differentiation, the things that will make you stand out from your perceived competition.

Differentiators That Work

- Easy or Simple – People are so busy that if you can demonstrate how easy it is to buy or use your product, or that it you can use it without reading a fifty page manual, people may respond to your message.

- Better value – Your product is comparatively priced with your competition but has additional features or appeal.

- Better features – This works if the features are something people want. If the features are something the average user of your product or service will use, they count. If they are just something to brag about, they won't

- Location – A good location that excludes your competition or brings you more traffic is a good thing. Beware however, if there's nothing stopping your competition from moving in across the street, you'll need something more than location alone unless it is usual or unique.

- Exclusivity – If you have a product that has patent or trade secret protections, this is a strong differentiator. The other kind of exclusivity, where the buyer has to have certain qualifications to purchase your product can also be effective, if those individuals want what you're selling.

Differentiators That Don't Work

- Quality – Most companies say the have the highest quality of whatever they make or do. This has been done so much that it really has become meaningless unless you are making something so high end and extraordinary that you don't need to say it's high quality, like a Rolls Royce.

- Lower Price – Unless you are Wal-Mart or Target, you do not want to compete by offering the lowest price. If your competition takes up the battle and also lowers their price it could very well be a race to the bottom with both of you losing. Remember, most consumers that come to you to get a lower price will leave you to get a lower price. Unless you're the 99 cent store, customers who buy on price are not your customers.

You want people who will pay a fair price for your product or service.

- Effective – Your product or service had better be effective or you won't be around long.

- Customer Service – Everyone says they care about their customers and deliver great customer service. If you're selling a spa experience, this is expected. If you're selling discount car stereos, people are focused on price. As a differentiator, you would have to be off the charts for this to pull. Think Ritz Carlton.

Competitive Landscape

The competitive landscape section of your marketing plan discusses your realistic local competition. For retail establishments this means businesses that offer similar services at similar price points to you that are within a five mile radius from you. This is because for most retail businesses, 80% of your business usually comes from within one mile of your store, 15% will come from within three miles and 5% will come from within five miles. The rules change a bit when there is a little more distance between competitors (as can be seen in our example) and you may need to push the borders out a little bit. For service businesses where the delivery area is bigger, then your competitive range will be larger and likely include more competition.

You don't have to do a lot of analysis on each competitor but you do have to try to find them and have some understanding of how they operate. From a survival sense, you should learn all about them: how they operate, how they market and how they price their products.

It's important to include only the businesses that are true competitors. If you are selling Hyundais, you are not competing with BMW dealers. You and your competition sell cars but to vastly different markets. You can have an American cuisine restaurant down the block from a high end French restaurant and have it not be competition, depending on how you view them.

This is important. Since you are trying to put the best face on your idea, you may be tempted to leave some competitors out of your analysis. If you do, make sure that they can't kill you. Make sure you are straight with yourself. We put every competitor in our plans and figure out how to beat them. That's the purpose of competitive analysis.

Below is an example of a competitive analysis. In this instance, we used Google maps to get the locations of other grooming establishments in our area by searching for 'pet grooming -animal hospitals'. That last part, the '-animal hospitals' eliminated animal hospitals from our search because we are choosing not to analyze them as competition. The reason for this is that animal hospitals are among the most expensive places you can get grooming services done and people who make that choice are likely doing so out of loyalty to the hospital. They are unlikely to switch to us.

The principal also chose not to place 'kennels' in the search because he knows the area and is fairly certain that Pet Palace is the only company within fifteen miles that has a doggie day care.

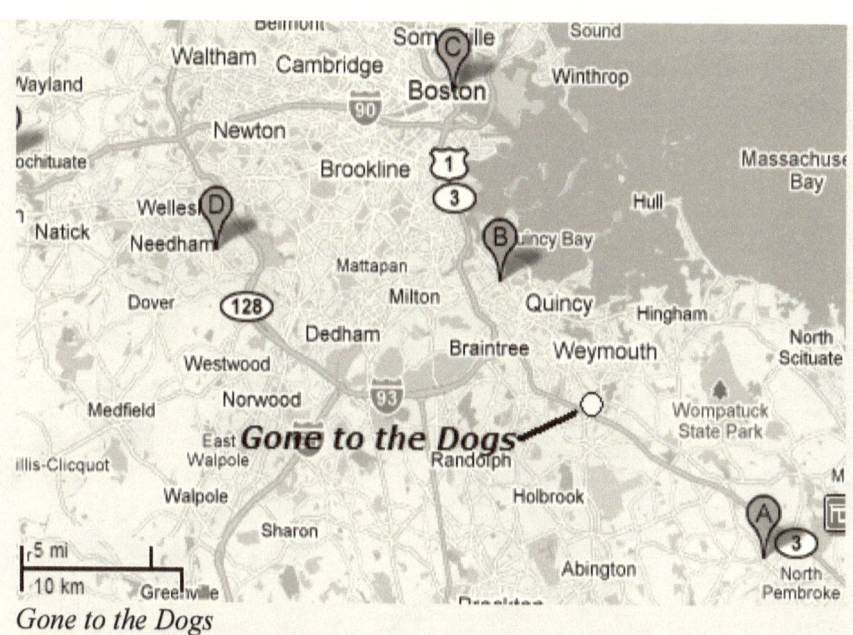

Gone to the Dogs

GTTD will be located in a strip mall along High Street (Route 3) in Concordia, MA. A Google Maps search reveals that there is little competition for the company in the immediate area:

A - Pet Palace - This establishment will be similar in its offerings to GTTD. The principal of GTTD was the manager of Pet Palace until

176

in addition to offering the same services as GTTD. It's been in business since 1955 and has an excellent reputation. It is also fifteen miles from GTTD and will not pose a serious threat to it. GTTD will likely draw some of the customers from it for grooming, since many customers from the Abington and Pembroke area take their animals there for service.

Not shown on the map:

There is a PetCo in Braintree that offers grooming services only. Because of the price difference between it and GTTD, it is not anticipated that PetCo customers would be GTTD customers.

There is a Pet City at Holbrook that offers grooming services. Pet City has been shut down four times by local authorities for unsanitary conditions and is held in low regard by the local population.

Gone to the Dogs did not analyze kennels as competition because the only local company that offers doggie day care is Pet Palace, discussed above.

Making Your Business Known to the Public

The key to making your business known to the public is an effective marketing campaign. You create this plan using the knowledge you have gained from your market research.

Strategy

There are only a few true marketing strategies. These strategies set the approach and tactics that you will use to promote your product. To a large degree, your strategy is set by your competition and their place in the market, as well as the nature and quality of your product. The primary strategies are:

Strategy	Characteristics	Notes
Direct	Overwhelmingly superior product or service Can be brought to market and scaled rapidly Uses mass market/saturation advertising techniques	It is an expensive strategy, used generally in national launches of products or services. Must be a new 'game changing' product like the iPad or an 'order of magnitude' improvement to an existing product.
Reposition	Provide a vastly improved product or service Change the rules of how a product or service is used Win over experts and opinion leaders Also uses mass market/saturation techniques	This strategy goes against the status quo and works by converting thought leaders to the new product. It is different from a fragmentation or niche strategy in that you are trying to move the majority of the market to your product as the ultimate goal of the strategy.
Fragment (Niche)	Divide and conquer market share based on differentiation Often incremental improvement	This is the strategy that you will be most likely using. Since most business start ups

	or added features are enough	are in existing industries, you will be emphasizing your superiority in terms of features or benefits.
	Mass marketing techniques are rarely employed	
	Message recipients are tightly targeted	

What is Branding?

Branding is marketing and advertising that is designed to associate your company with specific symbols, or logos, and tag lines. The objective is for the public, over time and exposure, to associate your brand with the logos and tag lines as an additional memory hook.

In the recent past, there was a lot of talk about how each person, even people attempting to land jobs, needed to brand themselves. Given that each one of us sees around 35,000 brand images every day, getting our brand noticed seems like a tall order. The branding discussion has moved back to a differentiation discussion. It is more important to stand out from your competition than to be identified with a symbol.

That does not mean that you should not have a logo or tag lines and that you should not strive to associate yourself with them. A well executed logo, when properly promoted, can become a short cut to your identity. It can replace the need for words when identifying your brand. People respond to logos and visuals generally, so it's a good idea to have them, if for nothing more than positioning for the future.

The iconic Nike swoosh was produced for $35. The company has spent billions promoting and defending it. It's one of the most recognized symbols in the world.

Also remember, that in the world of your customers and prospects, since they contact you directly and interact with you, your logo and tag line will have meaning.

Tactics

The marketing tactics chart below is intended to give you some ideas of why certain tactics are selected. Moving left to right, they describe tactics that are employed based on their approach and reach.

Approach	MASS				INDIVIDUAL
Reach	International	National	Regional	Local	Personal
Cost/Time	More Money				More Time
Customers	Easier to Get				Easier to Keep
Message	Branding ►◄		Branding/Benefits ►◄		Vanity/Features
Television	CNN/BBC/Cable	Broadcast Network Cable	Major Market Broadcast Cable	Local Station Cable	Low Watt Station Community Access Podcast
Radio		Satellite	Major Market Channel	Local Station	Podcast
Print	The Economist WSJ Time	WSJ/USAToday Time/Newsweek People/Us	LA Times/NY Times 'Living' Magazines Regional Editions	Local paper Coupon Clippers Stuffers	Door Hangers Trifolds Slip Sheets
Touch/ Networking	◄	Public Speaking Events and Seminars Trade associations Network Science	►	Chambers of Commerce Mixers Events/Seminars Public Speaking Volunteer Work	Appointments Meetings
Internet	All or Any, Depending on Targeting and Delivery				

The chart above describes several tactics that businesses use to raise customer awareness and places them in context regarding the approach and geographic reach of each. They are categories in terms of the audience they are trying to reach.

The first decision you must make, based on your customer identification work, is how you will target your customers. While most people think that targeting depends on dollars that is only partially true. It is also a function of who is likely purchase the product and how many of them will actually buy. It is primarily a choice made based on where you think you will find them.

Think about soap. Everyone uses soap. Some brands of soap are branded internationally. Saturation television, radio and print media campaigns are used. This is because billions of people buy soap. A small fraction of this market is worth many millions of dollars.

Now think about a luxury yacht. You've never seen one advertised on television, or radio. You may have seen a stock broker's distress sale in the Wall Street Journal or seen advertisements in magazines such as World Yachtman or The Robb Report. This is because the market for yachts is very small and consists of people who require a high degree of service. That is why most luxury yachts are sold by brokers who have standing relationships with clients and competitors.

When starting your business, it's safe to say that most of your marketing will be local and you should use the tactics that are appropriate for your market size.

For most small businesses, highly effective marketing is a make-or-break necessity. It's nearly impossible to be successful without good marketing and sales techniques. You've got to let people know about all the great things your business can provide to them, which means that your business must first provide those things that people are willing to pay for. That, in turn, means knowing who your customers are and getting so close to them that you can virtually anticipate their needs and desires.

Sale Funnels

While you won't include a sales funnel in your business plan, (but you could!) it's a good idea to start thinking in those terms. The sales funnel is a way to organize your thinking about how you process prospects or leads and turn them into sales. At minimum, a sales funnel consists of three major sections:

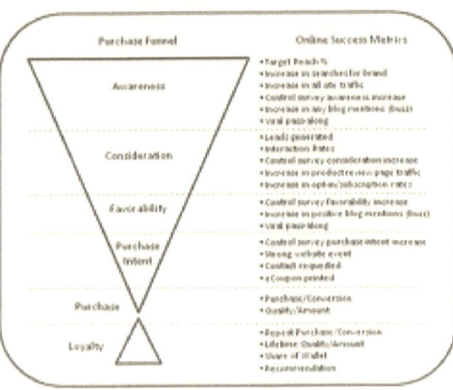

Awareness – During this stage all of the marketing efforts required to make prospective customers aware of your product occur. It can be anything from an e-mail offer to flyers to television advertising. The goal of this effort is to move the prospect to the next stage.

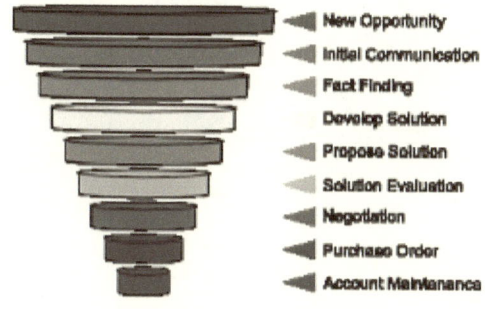

New Opportunity
Initial Communication
Fact Finding
Develop Solution
Propose Solution
Solution Evaluation
Negotiation
Purchase Order
Account Maintenance

Evaluation – Your prospect will test drive, comparison shop and educate themselves about your product in preparation of making a buying decision.

Action – This is the step you want to go your way, where the prospect buys your product and becomes a customer.

The sample funnels above have more steps based on the industry or product that they are selling. If you Google the words 'sales funnel', over 300,000 image results will come up, all variations of the same idea.

When you create your funnel, add the steps that are important to your sales process. Once you've created the funnel, identify the tasks and decisions that must take place in that stage. Doing so will make the selling process much clearer. It also helps identify the marketing tactics required. Focus on your conversion points for each stage of the funnel. The goal for each stage should be for a sales target to 'convert' or move to the next level of the funnel. Track your conversions to understand the success of your marketing work.

Marketing Schedule

A good way to budget for your marketing expense is to create a marketing schedule. Below is a sample marketing schedule for Gone to the Dogs. This form is available at *www.killerbusinessplan.com* by clicking on the 'Electronic Materials' on the menu bar. See *"How to Use this Book"* for more instructions.

	Jan	Feb	Mar	Apr	May	Jun	Jul	Aug	Sep	Oct	Nov	Dec
Offer/Product	Shampoozalosa	Basic Service	Basic Service	Shampoozalosa	Basic Service	Basic Service	Shampoozalosa	Basic Service	Basic Service	Basic Service	Shampoozalosa	Basic Service
Print	Clipper Magazine		Clipper Magazine	Weekly Newspaper Ad	Weekly Newspaper Ad Clipper Magazine	Weekly Newspaper Ad	Weekly Newspaper Ad Clipper Magazine		Clipper Magazine		Weekly Newspaper Ad Clipper Magazine	Weekly Newspaper Ad
Collateral	Cut sheets	Flyers	Flyers	Flyers	Flyers	Flyers	Flyers	Flyers	Flyers	Flyers	Flyers	Flyers
E-Mail - Offerings plus News	Weekly blast	Weekly blast	Weekly blast	Weekly blast	Weekly blast	Weekly blast	Weekly blast	Weekly blast	Weekly blast	Weekly blast	Weekly blast	Weekly blast
Events	Wine and Cheese mixer	I love my pet	Pet Safety	Wine and Cheese mixer	Play Date	Play Date	Wine and Cheese mixer	Play Date	Pet Safety	Wine and Cheese mixer	Pet holiday!	Holiday Mixer
Speaking			Pet Safety - Kiwanis	Radio Interview (Cost in spots)								
Radio				Care for your pet while on vacation spots	Care for your pet while on vacation spots	Care for your pet while on vacation spots					Holiday Specials	
Networking	Weekly Chamber breakfast	Weekly Chamber breakfast	Weekly Chamber breakfast	Weekly Chamber breakfast	Weekly Chamber breakfast	Weekly Chamber breakfast	Weekly Chamber breakfast	Weekly Chamber breakfast	Weekly Chamber breakfast	Weekly Chamber breakfast	Weekly Chamber breakfast	Weekly Chamber breakfast
Budget												
Print	800		800	650	1450	650	1450		800		1450	650
Collateral	150	25	25	25	25	25	25	25	25	25	25	25
E-Mail - Offerings plus News	20	20	20	20	20	20	20	20	20	20	20	20
Events	250	250	250	250	250	250	250	250	250	250	250	250
Speaking												
Radio				1200	1200	1200					1200	
Networking	20	20	20	20	20	20	20	20	20	20	20	20
Total Costs	1240	323	1123	2173	2973	2173	1773	323	1123	323	2973	973

Grand Total: 17,601

Across the top are the months of the year. Down the side are the various tactics that you have selected to market your business. The tactics we selected are for illustration purposes only; your tactics will be specific to your business. Below the grid that details the tactics is a corresponding grid that contains the costs for each tactic you employ. From this, you will get a total budget for the year. Be sure to go back and check this against the cash flow as your budget may have changed after you determined your strategy and approach. Below is a description of the line items of the form.

1. **Offer/Product** - This is the product or service you are promoting. As you can see in our example, Gone to the Dogs has a special promotion, 'Shampoozalosa', where they groom dogs for half price on a specific weekend once each quarter. The rest of the year, they are advertising their basic business.

   In practice, for every special offer you have, you would list it on this line.

2. **Print** – You add the names of the newspapers and publications you will be advertising in to support the offer. Below, in the budget section, put your cost estimate in.

3. **Collateral** – Any materials, such as flyers, catalogs or product specification sheets for example, are listed here. Remember to add the costs to your budget.

183

4. **Events** – If your business will hold open houses or other events, this is where you put them in your plan and budget.

5. **Speaking** – One of the most effective ways to advertise a business is through public speaking. List these events here along with any associated costs.

6. **Radio** – In this example, we're using radio, but it could be television or both.

7. **Networking** – These are occasions where you will be meeting people at events, such as chamber of commerce mixers, charity events and industry or trade association functions. If you were to join a professional networking organization, such as BNI, you would enter the dues and the monthly expenses in addition to costs for other events here.

Realize that your marketing schedule will be unique to your business. Take the categories offered as an example and a starting point.

Here are some marketing tactics that have proven useful for small businesses:

- Referrals. Actively encourage all satisfied customers as well as family and friends to refer to you people that could use your services. Give them all business cards. Remember to recognize people who refer you customers; you could offer a referral fee or at least send them a thank you note or email. If you have a website or do periodic email blasts, ask for testimonials to include in them.

  Building a referral business takes time. A lot of it. This is because referrals happen after you make sales not before, so you still have to get those first customers.

- Networking. Every time you are out of your house, think of yourself as in "business mode", and think of everyone you meet as a useful contact or potential customer. Always be prepared to sell yourself, and always have some business cards on you.

- One useful networking tool, depending on the age range and characteristics of your target market, are social networking sites like Facebook. By having a page for your business on one of these sites you can network with potential clients and gain some useful knowledge and insight about your target market.

- Become a member of your local chamber of commerce. This is a great place to network; you will meet many people that are potential customers or that will help you with your business. It will also give you good standing in the community, which means a positive image for potential customers.

- Website. Have a website for your business that is informative, well-designed and easy to use. Put the website URL on your business cards. Customers often like to research people they buy from before hand, and this will be helpful to them. Be sure to include contact information on the website. If possible offer some of your products for sale on your site.

- Consider using Youtube.com and Vimeo as a marketing tool. These websites are becoming more and more popular, and every day millions of people use them to research a variety of things, including products and services. Any commercials, instructional or informational videos you have can be uploaded to YouTube for millions of potential customers to view. Be sure to include a link to your website and/or a phone number for them to contact you.

- Take out ads in industry-specific magazines. For example, if you run an interior decorating business, take out an ad in a lifestyle magazine that other home improvement companies advertise in.

- If your budget allows, consider short commercials on local cable TV and radio channels. Be careful before you spend a lot of money on these options; choose the medium with caution, asking yourself "Who is the audience," and carefully craft the ad. Understand that this can become expensive, because radio and TV do not garner an immediate response. You may need to run your ad at least 12 weeks, the industry standard test period, before you begin to see results.

- Events – These are events you hold like seminars or networking events and events held by others you can attend such as city sponsored or charity events. Your local chamber of commerce and industry specific organizations also hold networking events.

- Networking Science-This focuses on extending your business through your personal contacts.

Network Science

Based on a mash up of computer networking theory and the concept of six degrees of separation, network science is an emerging theory of marketing. It's not a new idea. Last century, the same concept went under the name of *clout*, that is, the building and utilization of a group of contacts whom you could help and who could help you. The website LinkedIn is built on this concept.

The concept is fairly straight forward to describe, as discussed in the video below. You take an inventory of your contacts, categorizing them into the following groups: customers, prospects, allies and friends and family. You then list their contacts into the same categories to understand how their contacts align with your goal. Once completed, you will have a good idea of what your 1st, 2nd and 3rd degrees of separation look like.

You will be surprised at how close you are to some pretty important people. For example, because of one client, we are two degrees of separation from a president and two major media figures. A group of a half dozen clients put us within two degrees of the former governor of California, Arnold Schwarzenegger. We have a client that built armored limousines for a number of Hollywood celebrities. You'd be surprised at who they are.

This closeness may or may not translate into access. The quality of your contact's relationships and the willingness of your contact to link you to them will control your access. That's why analysis is critical. If you identify your target and the purpose for being introduced, it will make it easier for your contact to say yes.

Research into your target becomes very important to your success. You must first understand if your target will be sympathetic to your cause and if they have the ability to help you. You must make this determination because if your contact with the target appears to be a waste of time, then you will have little chance of reestablishing that connection later.

Your purpose can almost never be a sales pitch. You must find something that is compelling for the target that will also make your contact look good for connecting you. For example, the governor of my state is a man with a number of problems. He has a huge budget deficit gap to fill and declining tax revenues to do it. If I were attempting to get him to introduce me to various state agency heads to promote and sell my product, it's unlikely I'd get anymore than a chance at being in a photo with him. If however, I had an idea that could create a thousand jobs I would likely get his attention. Your pitch must relate to some problem or cause in your target's life or there is no reason for you to be connected to them.

Chapter 21 - Organizational Plan

The Goal of This Chapter

To understand what needs to be included in the organizational plan section of your business plan.

What You Will Do in This Chapter

Read the material on how to write the organizational plan section
Write the section

What You Will Have When You're Done

A completed organizational plan
Completed principals section

What is an Organizational Plan?

Organizational plans detail who will be part of the organization, who they report to and what authority they have. Obviously, a business employing a single person will be vastly simpler that one that employs hundreds. The basic elements of an organizational plan, at minimum are:

- An organizational chart detailing the lines of communication and authority (not necessary for very small businesses)
- The titles and roles of all management staff
- The titles and roles of line staff positions
- In the case of a company with a formal board of directors, a discussion of the board members and their qualifications
- Detailed biographies of the principals of the company

Who are the principals?

The principals of a company are the individuals that:

- Are the creators of the business idea and usually the owners if it is a small business
- Own significant equity in the new business
- Bring special knowledge or expertise that is critical to the success of the business. From a funding point of view, these are the people who will make the business succeed. The company would not be a good bet without these individuals. Since you're writing the plan, you are likely one of the principals.

Organization Chart

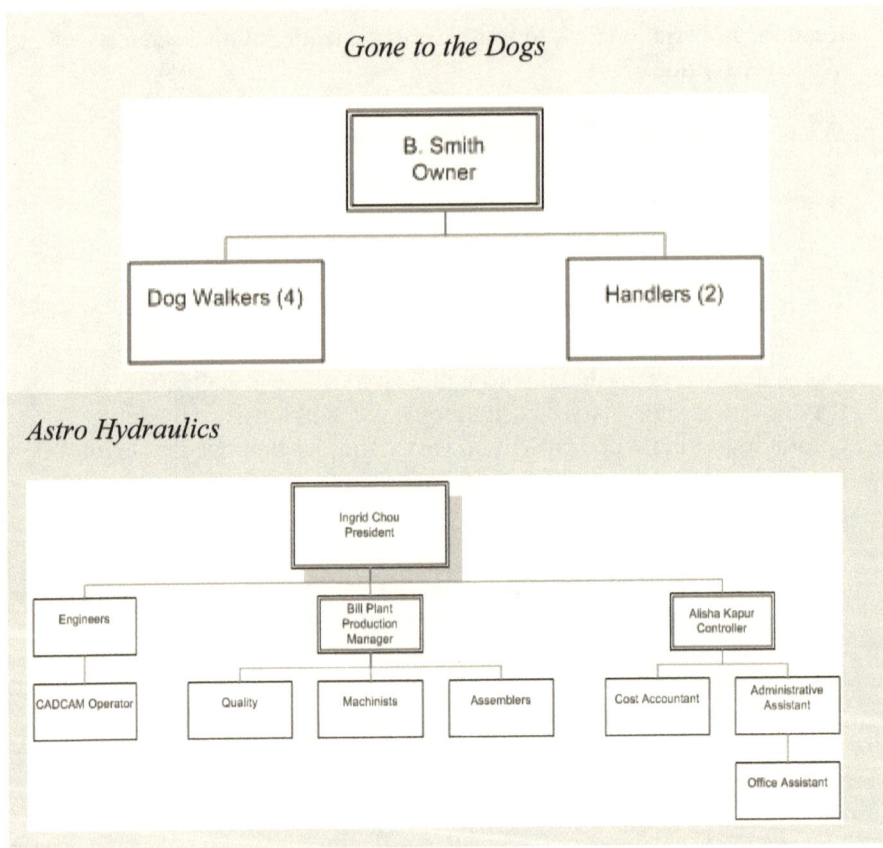

Titles and Roles of All Management Staff

Gone to the Dogs

The only management staff for this company is the owner. A description of his role and duties would look like this:
Company Management

Owner

The company will be managed by its owner, B. Smith. In this role he will be responsible for all human resources, purchase and operational decisions.

Astro Hydraulics

Astro Hydraulics has a more formal management team. Their paragraph could look something like this:
Company Management

President

Ingrid Chou has been President of Astro Hydraulics since it was purchased from the founder in 2003. Ms. Chou is responsible for all operations, sales and contract management with customers. She leads her design team through product development and improvement. Engineering and Production report directly to her.

Production Manager

Bill Plant is responsible for day to day operations of the manufacturing operations of Astro. Machining, Assembly, Test and Quality all report to Mr. Plant. He is responsible for all purchases for inventory and contract services. He also provides client troubleshooting support and is the point of contact for any issues with Astro's products. Mr. Plant also provides sales support when required.

Controller

Alisha Kapur is the Controller of Astro. Her responsibilities include all financial reporting, oversight of the company's accounting systems, review and approval of all major purchases and contracts.

On Your Side

Given that On Your Side has only one employee, general practice is not to have any discussion before the write up of the company principals.

Titles and Roles of Staff Positions

Gone to the Dogs
Dog Walkers visit pets that are left at home by their owners while on travel or because they have long commutes. They walk the dog, check the pet's food and water and play with the animal during the visit. The walker leaves a report for the pet's owner which is a two part form, one copy coming back to the company for quality control purposes.

Handlers work in the store and check pets in and out each day. They feed and water the animals and exercise them several times a day. They also handle all merchandise sales. They monitor the pets for any unusual behavior and report to the owner if necessary.

Groomers work as contractors, they only go to the center when they have scheduled appointments. They groom the dogs, bathe them, trim their nails, comb them and brush their teeth.

Astro Hydraulics
The **Cost Accountant** is responsible for tracking purchases and time recorded for various manufacturing steps to allow for the build up of unit cost for products made by the company. The Cost Accountant also audits department performance as directed by the Controller. Reports to the Controller.

Engineers are responsible for the design and test of company products as well designing the required tooling needed to produce component parts. They also work with the quality department by sampling and checking parts as they are made. Reports to the President.

CADCAM Operator creates the drawings and bills of material for all products made by the company on the company's AutoCAD system. The CADCAM Operator is also responsible for maintenance of the company's computer systems and network. Reports to Engineering.

Administrative Assistant provides support to all staff as well as receiving all accounts receivable and payable and entering them into the company's accounting software. Reports to the Controller

Office Assistant performs duties as assigned. Reports to the Administrative Assistant.

Board of Directors

Astro Hydraulics Only
Astro Hydraulics has a five member Board of Directors that is responsible for setting company strategy, approving major capital purchases as well as approving the hiring, termination and compensation of executives. The board consists of the investors who purchased Astro from its founder in 2003. The board meets once a quarter in person and has teleconferences once each month to discuss progress against plan and to deal with issues that have arisen. The Board is available on short notice for emergencies.

At the beginning of each fiscal year, the Board reviews and approves an annual operating plan and budget submitted by the management team.

Board Membership

Ingrid Chou – President (see principals for a discussion of Ms. Chou's qualifications).

Ralph Dunderan – A former owner of seven different contract machine and manufacturing shops, he has extensive experience with the aerospace industry. He has invested in several manufacturing start ups.

Wilma Bryce – Ms. Bryce is a principal with Swiftwater Funds, a venture capital firm that invests in technology and defense businesses. She represents Swiftwater's interests in the firm.

Phillip White – Mr. White has worked as a maintenance supervisor for American Airlines and currently owns Sacony Aviation, a repair station specializing in private jets.

Wyatt Connors – With over 40 years of senior management experience in the aerospace industry and two successful aerospace startups to his credit, Mr. Connors provides frequent management support in addition to his duties on the Board of Directors.

Principals

Gone to the Dogs

B Smith- the principal of Gone to the Dogs has 15 years of experience in pet care. Starting in high school, B. Smith had held several positions in Petco including stock person, cashier, groomer, assistant manager and manager. After working for Petco for 8 years, B. Smith took a position with Pet Palace, a boarding kennel, as manager.

At Pet Palace, B. Smith was responsible for most aspects of the operation, as the owner only came in every 2 weeks to pay bills and write payroll checks. Advertising, hiring, firing, training, overseeing grooming operations, customer service and scheduling employees were her main duties performed at Pet Palace.

B Smith's responsibilities at Petco and Pet Palace have provided a firm foundation of knowledge and experience that will be invaluable when starting "Gone to the Dogs".

Astro Hydraulics

I. Chou first came to work for Astro Hydraulics as a cad cam operator while finishing her engineering degree at UCI (University of California Irvine). Once she earned her degree in 1985 she was promoted to engineer. During this time she was responsible for testing company products and after 2 years, was promoted to designing products for Astro Hydraulics. Ms. Chou earned her MBA from Pepperdine University in 1992 and took a position with Cessna Aircraft company in Wichita, Kansas.

While at Cessna Ms. Chou held a variety of positions starting in the engineering department and moving to supply chain and finally manufacturing where the last position held was Vice President with responsibilities for Manufacturing Technical Services (MTS). MTS is a multi-discipline engineering organization responsible for providing technical support to the manufacturing and product engineering functions within Cessna.

In 2001 Ms. Chou, having maintained a relationship with her past employer, was contacted by the owner of Astro Hydraulics and asked if she would be interested in purchasing the business. In 2003 a group of investors including Ms. Chou purchased Astro Hydraulics.

On Your Side

Joining AT&T in 1979 Mr. Roberts has held positions in network operations, marketing and sales. The contacts made during his years in corporate America are part of what makes his business unique. He has industry experts at his fingertips that he can use to help his customers grow with their businesses.

Mr. Roberts retired after 30 years at AT&T. During his tenure he held positions of increasing responsibility, the last being Executive Vice President of Sales. Choosing to be near family members, Mr. Roberts moved to Del Rio, Texas. He will begin helping small business owners become more successful beginning in 2011.

Outside Consultants/Advisors

These are the people who will help assure your success. If you have a mentor or a business consultant their information should be added here. Your accountant or bookkeeper or lawyer would also be appropriate here. If you are looking for an investor, and you are working with a venture capital firm, the firm's information would be here.

Gone to the Dogs

The only advisor for this company is an accountant who will also handle the monthly bookkeeping.

Outside Consultants/Advisors

Michael Trent- Owner
We do Taxes and Bookkeeping
38864 N.E. 15th Street
Concordia, MA 01221

Chapter 22 - Executive Summary

The Goal of This Chapter

Learn how to write an effective Executive Summary

What You Will Do in This Chapter

Read the material on how to write an executive summary
Write your executive summary

What You Will Have When You're Done

A completed executive summary

How Do I Write My Executive Summary?

The Executive Summary is a brief synopsis at the beginning of a business plan that highlights key facts, issues, and conclusions. The executive summary is your three-minute window of opportunity. It is the place where people decide if they want to read the rest of your plan. It is your opportunity to make a compelling argument for what your company does, to position it within its competitive landscape and to demonstrate why your company will rise above others to challenge what exists and become the leader in its field. Be brief. One to two pages is ample space to get your point across.

The executive summary should always be written last. The reason being, you are summarizing everything covered in your plan. While you write and develop your narrative, information may change or the theme might shift. Save yourself time and hassle by writing the executive summary last, referring to the rest of your completed narrative to guide you.

Things to Consider Including in Your Executive Summary

- Company name, address and year founded

- Brief background of owner including any relevant experience or degrees

- Information about your company's purpose as well as future plans

- How your business stands out from the competition

- Ways in which you will market your business to the consumer

- Some brief industry research

- Any relevant information that supports the existence of your business

Gone to the Dogs

Gone to the Dogs (GTTD) will be a full service dog day care and grooming center that will also provide in home visits for pets left at home by owners on travel or those that have long daily commutes. Based in a 2,600 sq. ft. commercial retail space near the upscale neighborhood of Harbor Isle in Concordia, MA, GTTD will have six to ten employees delivering in home pet visits, doggy day care, grooming services and selling pet food and merchandise.

The business will initially be open 68 hours per week to cover the commuter patterns of the community. It is estimated that the company will be able to serve about two hundred unique customers per year with this level of transactions enabling the company to meet it pro forma financial projections.

The pet care industry was projected to reach $47.7 BN in revenue in 2010. Pet services, which consist of grooming and boarding, are projected to be $3.45BN. Despite the recent recession, this segment of the industry continues to grow. 62% of all American households have pets with 46.6 million homes having at least one dog. In Massachusetts, the market was $68.6 MM in 2007. Gone to the Dogs will offer high touch, customer and pet services that take advantage of emerging and existing trends in the industry:

Pet's well being is being taken into account by their owners: Once animals were left at home or put in kennels when their owners were traveling. Pet hotels, spas and toy gyms have sprung into being to pamper pets.

Owners are demanding human quality food and services for their animals: Most owners want their pets to have healthy food to eat. They want grooming and medical services to keep their companions healthy.

Designers and big brand companies are moving into the pet space: Many larger retailers and pet food producers are moving into mid and upper priced offerings that provide more selection and higher quality.

Despite the decline in incomes, owners are dedicating more of their disposable income on their pets: Pets are seen as companions and family members, now more than ever. Owners are choosing to take better care of their animals.

B. Smith will be the owner/operator of Gone to the Dogs. He has 15 years of experience in pet care having worked with Petco for eight years in positions of increasing responsibility, ending up as store manager. He then managed a boarding kennel, Pet Palace, where he had full operational responsibility for the business as the owner was not involved in daily operations. The company projects it will earn first year revenues of $499K with earnings before interest and tax of $179K at a margin of 36%.

Financial Needs

This section will have clear statements concerning how much money you will need to launch the business and a breakdown of how the funds will be allocated. The line items identified here will be capital (big ticket) purchases including machinery, furniture, computer equipment and tenant improvements. If you are purchasing a business you still want to allocate the funds so the bank or your investor knows how much money is being used for inventory, machinery, vehicles, etc.

Gone to the Dogs

Gone to the Dogs will be leasing space in a commercial retail space located in a strip mall. The space has been leased before, so it already has some improvements including space for an office and public restrooms. The tenant improvements will include tearing down walls, installing the kennels, upgrading the air conditioning and laying down a special rubberized floor in the dog play area. Their financial needs looks like this:

Tenant Improvements	
Demolition and construction of walls	$5,500
Air Conditioning Upgrades	3,500
Rubberized Floor 1,000 sq ft x $3.00	3,000
Kennels to house 100 dogs	13,500
Dog Washing/Grooming Stations (2)	5,000
Dog Washing Accessories (dryers, clippers)	3,500
Point of Sale (POS) System	3,500
Merchandise and Toys	10,000
Dog Food and Treats	8,000
Phone/Intercom System	4,500
Security Cameras and Web Cams	2,500
Office Furniture	5,500
Office Computer Equipment	2,500
Web Site Build	5,000
Working Capital (6 mos of expenses)	100,634
Total Funds Needed	$176,134
Owner Injection	26,134
Funds Requested	$150,000

At a Glance

The business plan template provided to you includes a section called "At a Glance". This section provides a brief overview of the business discussed in the plan. It gives the reader the high points including the industry and market of the business, information on the owner and a high level look at the functional roles of the employees. Any areas that don't apply to your specific situation you can leave blank or put N/A in the field.

People love this chart because it contains many important business facts in one place that is easy to find.

Gone to the Dogs At a Glance

Legal Name	Gone to the Dogs	
Location:	1345 S. Route 3 Concordia, MA 01221	
Type of Business	Limited Liability Company (LLC)	
Date Incorporated	June 2010	
NAICS Code	812910 Pet Care Services	
Owner	B. Smith	
Primary Contact	B. Smith	
Contact Number	(888) 199-4562	
Shares Outstanding	N/A	
Business Activity	Dog services: boarding, sitting, and grooming Retail sales	
Markets	Households with incomes of 100K or more	
Trends	Many pet owners are pampering their pets and consider them a "family member" Owners are demanding human quality food and services for their animals Increasing demand for day care and hotel services for pets	
Selling Methods	Direct sales	
Seasonality	Holidays and Summer	
Employees	Title	Functional Roles
	Manager	Responsible for all human resources, purchase and operational decisions Oversees the day to day operations.
	Dog walker	Visits the dogs at their houses twice a day
	Handlers	Sale the products and services Check pets in and out Monitor and take care of the pets
	Groomers	Bathes and clips dogs
Labor Supply	Adequate labor is available in the immediate area	
Facility	2,600 sq. ft. commercial retail space 1345 S. Route 3 Concordia, MA 01221	
Legal	No legal action is pending. The company has no judgments against it.	

Chapter 23 - Document Assembly

The Goal of This Chapter

Compile the different sections into a finished business plan

What You Will Do in This Chapter

Put the finishing touches on your completed business plan

What You Will Have When You're Done

A finished, professional looking business plan

How Should I Package It?

Creating a professional looking package can sometimes be as important as the content within. Many bankers and potential investors want to see a professional looking plan containing a coversheet, table of contents, and header/ footer with company name and page numbers on each page.

The cover sheet can include the full legal name of your corporation or business, address, phone number, web site, and name and title of the person to contact at your company, with specific e-mail and phone contact information. Ideally, place each piece of information on a separate line and center it in the middle of your cover page. Use a large font. You may wish to include your company logo as well. If you do not have a company logo, find a picture or image that is relevant to place on the center of your cover page, generally taking up the middle third of the page, above the contact information.

Staple the cover sheet to your narrative and financials if you intend to include them. For the full plan, consider a clear plastic sheet over the cover page with spiral binding connecting it to a vinyl sheet on the back. Placing the plan in a binder works as well if you place the cover sheet on the front with the rest of the narrative inside.

To others, a business plan will be the best indicator that can be used to judge your potential for success. It should be no more than 20 to 40 pages in length, excluding supporting documents. If you are seeking a lender or investor: Include only the supporting documents that will be of immediate interest to the person examining your plan. Keep the others with your own copy where they will be available on short notice. You can have your plan neatly bound at your local print shop or purchase covers from a local stationery or office supply store.

Glossary

A

ACS (American Community Survey) – This is a survey used by the U.S. Census bureau to get demographic data. It is sent to a small percentage of the population on a rotating basis. The purpose of the ACS is to get information about the changing population for the time periods in between the U.S. Census, which is only conducted every 10 years. The data obtained using the ACS is used to help make decisions on policies, programs, and services for communities in the United States, determining how $300 billion in tax dollars is spent every year.

Assets - Something of value that a firm owns or controls. Examples include: cash, inventory equipment, property, patents or goodwill.

B

Balance Sheet – The financial statement of a business or institution that lists the assets, debts and owner's investment on a specific date. Assets = Liabilities + Owner's Equity

Breakeven - The level of output or sales necessary to cover fixed expenses. The break-even point (BEP) is the point at which cost or expenses and income are equal: there is no net loss or gain, and one has "broken even".

Business Model - Description of means and methods a firm employs to earn the revenue projected in its plans. It views the business as a system and answers the question, "How are we going to make money to survive and grow?"

C

Capacity - Specific ability of an entity (person or organization) or resource, measured in quantity and level of quality, over an extended period.

Capital - Wealth in the form of money or property, used or accumulated in a business by a person, partnership, or corporation. Material wealth used or available for use in the production of more wealth.

Collateral - Assets pledged as security for a loan. In the event of borrower default on the terms of a loan, the collateral may be sold, with proceeds used to satisfy any remaining obligations. High-quality collateral reduces risk to the lender and results in a lower rate of interest on the loan.

Competitors - The competitors of a company, are usually in the same industry, and are striving to secure the business of a similar group of consumers by offering them products and services with similar terms.

Cost - The amount of money or use of property needed to produce a product or service.

Cost of Goods Sold (COGS) - The cost of purchasing materials and preparing goods for sale. Also known as *'Direct Expense'*.

Customer – A group of consumers that share common needs or characteristics and are most likely to buy your products or services.

D

Differentiation - Result of efforts to make a product or brand stand out as a provider of unique value in comparison with its competition.

Dream Book – A notebook of blank pages used to collect your ideas and inspirations and details of things you like for your business. This could include newspapers or magazine articles and clippings, photos or illustrations.

Debt Service - Funds required to meet interest expenses and/or principal payments.

Demographics - Socioeconomic groups, characterized by age, income, sex, education, occupation, etc., that comprise a market niche.

Depreciation - The periodic cost assigned for the reduction in usefulness and value of a long-term tangible asset.

Dilution - A decrease in the equity position (value) of a share of stock because of the issuance of additional shares. Dilution is usually detrimental to the position of existing shareholders because it weakens their proportional claim on earnings and assets.

Direct cost - A cost that can be directly related to producing specific goods or performing a specific service. For example, the wages of an employee engaged in producing a product can be attributed directly to the cost of manufacturing the product. Certain other costs such as depreciation and administrative expenses are more difficult to assign and are not considered direct costs.

Due Diligence - Is a term used for a number of concepts involving either an investigation of a business or person prior to signing a contract, or an act with a certain standard of care.

E

EBIT - Earnings Before Interest & Tax shows the company's earnings after expenses but before interest and taxes.

Executive Summary - A short document that summarizes a longer report, proposal or group of related reports in such a way that readers can rapidly become acquainted with a large body of material without having to read it all. It will usually contain a brief statement of the problem or proposal covered in the major document(s), background information, concise analysis and main conclusions.

Expenses - Money spent to operate the business NOT directly related to producing product for sale. Rent, telephone, insurance and advertising are all examples of expenses. Also known as *'Indirect Expense'*.

F

Financial Projections - See *Pro Forma Cash Flow*

Full Time Equivalent - Is a way to measure a worker's involvement in a project, or a student's enrollment at an educational institution.

G

Geographics - The analysis of geographic (location-based) information to improve business processes, acquire customers, manage growth and make more informed decisions.

Goal - A projected state of affairs that a person or a system plans or intends to achieve; a personal or organizational desired end-point.

Gross Profit - Revenue – COGS = Gross Profit, does not include income from incidental sources or selling and administrative expenses.

H

Hockey Stick - A revenue projection named for the shape of a hockey stick. Revenues are near zero or flat until a specific event, such as a product introduction or marketing campaign. This event causes revenues to rise steeply and continuously.

I

Indirect Cost - A cost that is not directly related to the production of a specific good or service but that is indirectly related to a variety of goods or services. For example, the cost of administering a large company is an indirect cost that must be spread over a number of products or services. Also known as *'Overhead'*.

Industry - A group of companies offering products or services that are close substitutes and that satisfy the same basic customer needs.

L

Liabilities – Future obligations to pay an amount in money, goods or services to another party. Examples include: leases, long-term debt, wages and taxes payable, and accounts payable.

M

Marketing - The process of identifying a target consumer for your product or service and creating the message, strategy and tactics to reach them.

Market Research - The systematic, objective collection and analysis of data about a particular target market, competition, and/or environment. The purpose of market research is to achieve an increased understanding of your target market, your industry and your competitors.

Mission Statement - Is a formal, short, written statement of the purpose of a company or organization. The mission statement should guide the actions of the organization, spell out its overall goal, provide a sense of direction, and guide decision making.

N

NAICS (North American Industry Classification System) - NAICS replaces the SIC (Standard Industry Classification). NAICS was developed as the standard for use by federal statistical agencies in classifying business establishments for the collection, analysis, and publication of statistical data related to the business economy of the U.S. It provides comparability in statistics about business activity across North America.

Net Income – Income after all expenses (fixed and variable) and taxes have been deducted. Net income is the most frequently viewed figure in a firm's financial statements.

Net Operating Income – Income from ordinary business activities minus expenses. It excludes interest, taxes and nonrecurring items such as losses from closing a plant.

O

Overhead – See *Indirect Cost*

P

Price - The quantity of one thing that is exchanged or demanded in barter or sale for another.

Process - An ordered set of events required to achieve a repeatable, quality result.

Profit and Loss Statement - It is a business financial statement that lists revenues, expenses and net income throughout a given period. Also known as *'Income Statement'*.

Pro Forma Cash Flow - A financial statement prepared on the basis of some assumed events and transactions that have not yet occurred. Also known as *'Financial Projections'*.

Product Development Cycle - Period of time needed to complete the set of events that develops an idea into a quality product. This time is broken into the following phases; generate the idea, plan, develop, validate, qualify and produce the end product.

Psychographics - Analysis of consumer lifestyles to create a detailed customer profile. Market researchers conduct psychographic research by asking consumers to agree or disagree with activities, interests, opinions statements. Results of this exercise are combined with geographic (place of work or residence) and demographic (age, education, occupation, etc.) characteristics to develop a more 'lifelike' portrait of the targeted consumer segment.

R

Revenue – Money coming into your business from selling goods or services.

Revenue Stream - The income obtained from a particular source or activity.

S

Sales - The activities involved in directly selling products or services to the consumer in return for money or other compensation.

Strategy - A long term plan of action designed to achieve a particular goal (a desired state), most often "winning".

SWOT Analysis - Is a strategic planning method used to evaluate the Strengths, Weaknesses, Opportunities, and Threats involved in a project or in a business venture.

T

Tactics - Methods or actions used to implement a strategy.

U

Underwriter - An individual responsible for reviewing a bank loan application and determining if it qualifies and is profitable enough for consideration by the bank.

V

Vision Statement – Aspirational description of what an organization would like to achieve or accomplish in the mid-term or long-term future. It is intended to serves as a clear guide for choosing current and future courses of action. See also *Mission Statement*.

Index

Want more information and assistance from the authors of 'Killer Business Plan'?

Business Plan Review and Comment

Would you like a professional review of your business plan?

Would you feel more comfortable if your plan had been reviewed by professionals before being presented to a bank or investor?

- We will review your plan for clarity, readability, completeness and suitability for purpose.
- We will provide written comments for adjustments.
- If there is something crucial missing, we'll give you detailed information on how include it.

Get useful feedback today! Call 800-741-8444

Advice and Accountability

Don't want to go it alone?

As an option, you can choose to have us guide you step-by-step through the planning process. We will answer your questions and help you work your way through your business plan on an agreed upon schedule.

Get the help you need today! Call 800-741-8444

Want a Professional Business Plan Written for You?

We have written plans for start-ups, franchises, purchases and expansions. We create original, affordable, custom business plans because your talent, experience and energy are one of a kind. Your plan will be specific to you.

After all, we wrote the book on creating a *Killer Business Plan.*

Get started today! Call 800-741-8444